The
WOMB
of
PRAYER

FRANCIS B. THOMAS

ISBN: 9798666228258
Published by

www.improved2life.com

To Contact the Author

Bishop Francis B. Thomas

World Resurrection Ministries Inc.
4117 Woerner Avenue
Levittown, PA 19057

Phone: 267-709-0723

Email: francisbthomas@yahoo.com

TABLE OF CONTENTS

◆◆◆◆◆◆◆◆◆◆◆◆◆◆◆◆

THE WOMB OF PRAYER

◆◆◆◆◆◆◆◆◆◆◆◆◆◆◆◆◆◆

The wind blew ferociously and it seemed like the roofs of the houses everywhere would be blown off. December had arrived once again, and it was harmattan season. The streets were empty; children were told to get off the street.

It was six o'clock in the evening, and I was at the front door of our house waiting for my friends so we could make our way to the nightclub. I was a teen and in the tenth grade   I was excited about the evening because my mother had consented to me going to my friend's place to do my homework. She did not know that I was going to the nightclub.

While waiting for my friends, I had a quick opportunity to go to our next-door neighbor to ask for some money. While I was in the house of our next-door neighbor, my friends had passed by and were not patient enough to wait for me, so the three of them left without me. I was furious and frustrated. Why would they do this?

1

Since I did not want to go by myself, I returned to my neighbor's house to watch the soccer match on their television. I was not interested in the game, but I wanted to stay away before going home. I did not want to go home and tell my mom that I did not go do my homework. We were twenty minutes into the game when I heard that my friends had just been involved in a ghastly motor accident. I was shocked beyond anything.

I quickly ran back to the house and loudly called my mom, but there was no answer. Wondering why she did not respond, I walked to her room and found her on her knees praying, sweating, and crying at the same time. She was saying, "I thank you for saving my son. I thank you because your banner over us is love."

I stood at the door not wanting to disturb her, and I was compelled to wait until she was done. I said, "Mom, there is something that I need to tell you." She sat up. I said, "You know I lied to you that I was going to do my homework, but I was planning with my friends to go to a nightclub.

She said, "I knew that because God told me you were in danger so I decided to spend the time praying for you." I told her my friends had an accident on the freeway and I was not sure they would survive. I dropped on my knees before her with tears in my eyes telling her how grateful I was to have a praying mother like her. This was my first introduction to the world of prayers.

Many books have been written over the years on the topic of prayer. Prayer is as old as creation itself. Prayer is the power of this present world and the world that is to come. The most single powerful tool given to humanity on this planet is prayer. If we take a critical look at every religion in the world, we will realize that prayer is what fuels their energy.

Maybe one of the honest questions we must ask ourselves is: "Where did the idea of prayer come from, and why do men pray? Maybe we need to face some realities here. Prayer is not a relic but a human thing. Everyone prays for something. Even an atheist prays to his atheism. Another question we must ask ourselves is: "How did we inherit the DNA and chromosome of prayer? Why do we have prayer in our genetic formulas and makeup?

In order to answer these questions, we need to look at the book of the beginning of every beginning - the book of Genesis.

In the beginning, God created heaven and the earth. He also made man in His image and in His likeness.

Genesis 1:26-28 King James Version (KJV)

> **26** And God said, Let us make man in our image, after our likeness: and let them have dominion over the fish of the sea, and over the fowl of the air, and over the cattle, and

overall the earth, and over every creeping thing that creepeth upon the earth.

27 So God created man in his own image, in the image of God created him; male and female created he them.

28 And God blessed them, and God said unto them, Be fruitful, and multiply, and replenish the earth, and subdue it: and have dominion over the fish of the sea, and over the fowl of the air, and over every living thing that moveth upon the earth.

The story of creation was properly documented in the Bible. Historical records and archeological facts had established these documents for thousands of years. So therefore, if we were made in the image and likeness of God, our tendency to pray must be coming from God. Just as we all have the likeness of His tendency to love, to care, to work, to create, to be jealous, and to feel. I believe and submit to you that God is a praying God. He made what He made on this planet by praying.

First and foremost let us look at the definition of prayer. **Prayer** can be **defined** as talking to **God**, Prayer can also be defined as speaking, saying words of wish, and supplication. A prayer is an act of talking to God, but it is much more than that. **A prayer** is an act of worship that glorifies **God** and reinforces our need for Him. Through living a life of **prayer**, we respond to Christ's work of salvation and communicate with the very source and purpose for our existence. Prayer can also be speaking forth, saying the word. So if prayer is all of these and we likened God to Him praying, the question then will be, who was He speaking to at the point of creation? In order to answer that question, we need to go back to the book of Genesis.

Genesis 1:26-28 King James Version (KJV)

> **26** And God said, Let us make man in our image, after our likeness: and let them have dominion over the fish of the sea, and over the fowl of the air, and over the cattle, and over all the earth, and over every creeping thing that creepeth upon the earth.
>
> **27** So God created man in his own image, in the image of God created he him; male and female created he them

Genesis 2:7 King James Version (KJV)

> **7** And the Lord God formed man of the dust of the ground, and breathed into his nostrils the breath of life; and man became a living soul.

We all know from this text that God Himself made man without help from an outsider. We also know that He was speaking to the gathering of His council. He went ahead and made man in His image and likeness even though He informed His council. God has

His council. I know with this statement, I must have created some tensions. Like many of you, I used to think that God had nothing else but Himself. I also used to think when the Bible speaks about other gods, it was just for speaking sake and there was none.

However, after thirty years, I realized that the Bible will never say other gods if there were no other gods. I also realized that in order for me to get an understanding of the Bible, I must have the mind of the ancient writers. The manuscripts that were authenticated by the Septuagint were written by the ancient authors of the Old Testament. If you are an addicted believer of the Bible like me and you are reading this book, then you will believe everything written in the Bible. Let us explore:

Psalm 82 King James Version (KJV)

> **82** God standeth in the congregation of the mighty; he judgeth among the gods.

This text shows that God had company before the creation, and from all indications, they were His family. A family that will on the last day be united with the ones on earth and we all shall be one. That is the reason why the ultimate redemption of humanity was wrought by Jesus Christ. We must also be clear that God does not need a council to do anything, but He chose to have one. God does not need humans to do whatever He needs to do, but He made us.

Job 1:6-8

> **6** Now there was a day when the sons of God came to present themselves before the Lord, and Satan came also among them.
>
> **7** And the Lord said unto Satan, Whence comest thou? Then Satan answered the Lord, and said, From going to and fro in the earth, and from walking up and down in it.
>
> **8** And the Lord said unto Satan, Hast thou considered my servant Job, that there is none like him in the earth, a perfect and an upright man, one that feareth God, and escheweth evil?.

God also asked Job some questions that showed He had a company that celebrated when He was done with the creation.

Job 38:4-7 King James Version (KJV)

> **4** Where wast thou when I laid the foundations of the earth? declare, if thou hast understanding.
>
> **5** Who hath laid the measures thereof, if thou knowest? or who hath stretched the line upon it?
>
> **6** Whereupon are the foundations thereof fastened? or who laid the cornerstone thereof;
>
> **7** When the morning stars sang together and all the sons of God shouted for joy?

We must however be definitely clear that God may have informed His council in advance, but none of them was there when He got to work at the creation. As He gets done, the master architect presented His creation to Himself and said it was good. And of course, His council celebrated for joy and gave praise to Him who lives and abides forever.

Psalm 89:5-7 King James Version (KJV)

> **5** And the heavens shall praise thy wonders, O Lord: thy faithfulness also in the congregation of the saints.
> **6** For who in the heaven can be compared unto the Lord? who among the sons of the mighty can be likened unto the Lord?
> **7** God is greatly to be feared in the assembly of the saints, and to be had in reverence of all them that are about him

Let us explore more Scriptures:

1 Kings 22:14-22 King James Version (KJV)

> **14** And Micaiah said, As the Lord liveth, what the Lord saith unto me, that will I speak.
> **15** So he came to the king. And the king said unto him, Micaiah, shall we go against Ramothgilead to battle, or

shall we forbear? And he answered him, Go, and prosper: for the Lord shall deliver it into the hand of the king.

16 And the king said unto him, how many times shall I adjure thee that thou tell me nothing but that which is true in the name of the Lord?

17 And he said, I saw all Israel scattered upon the hills, as sheep that have not a shepherd: and the Lord said, these have no master: let them return every man to his house in peace.

18 And the king of Israel said unto Jehoshaphat, Did I not tell thee that he would prophesy no good concerning me, but evil?

19 And he said, Hear thou, therefore, the word of the Lord: I saw the Lord sitting on his throne, and all the host of heaven standing by him on his right hand and on his left.

20 And the Lord said, Who shall persuade Ahab, that he may go up and fall at Ramoth gilead? And one said on this manner, and another said on that manner.

21 And there came forth a spirit, and stood before the Lord, and said, I will persuade him.

22 And the Lord said unto him, Wherewith? And he said, I will go forth, and I will be a lying spirit in the mouth of all his prophets. And he said, Thou shalt persuade him, and prevail also: go forth and do so.

It is very clear from this passage that God has a council. I do not intend to delve into the nitty-gritty and exegesis of this text, my aim is just to draw your attention to the validity of my premise. Let us not forget that there is a reason why God kept all these passages in the Bible. Now in order not to be judged by many theologians as being lopsided in my analysis, I like to add a few New Testament passages that lend credence to the issue of God, His council, man, and His creation.

1 Peter 3:18-22 King James Version (KJV)

> **18** For Christ also hath once suffered for sins, the just for the unjust, that he might bring us to God, being put to death in the flesh, but quickened by the Spirit:
>
> **19** By which also he went and preached unto the spirits in prison;
>
> **20** Which sometime were disobedient when once the longsuffering of God waited in the days of Noah, while the ark was a preparing, wherein few, that is, eight souls were saved by water.
>
> **21** The like figure whereunto even baptism doth also now save us (not the putting away of the filth of the flesh, but the answer of a good conscience toward God,) by the resurrection of Jesus Christ:

22 Who is gone into heaven, and is on the right hand of God; angels and authorities and powers being made subject unto him.

Jude 5-6 King James Version (KJV)

5 I will therefore put you in remembrance, though ye once knew this, how that the Lord, having saved the people out of the land of Egypt, afterward destroyed them that believed not.

6 And the angels which kept not their first estate, but left their own habitation, he hath reserved in everlasting chains under darkness unto the judgment of the great day.

As I said, God created all things by the power of His word, and this was done by the essence of praying Himself to it. Now I had made it clear based on scripture that God spoke to His council about making, but He alone did the making. For example, I could sit down with my pastors and say to them, "Let us go have lunch", and they all follow me; but I, and I alone, provided the lunch. Yes, they were informed but could do nothing until I got it done. God said, "Let us…", but He alone went to do it because none of them had the power to do it. God alone brought creation to being without any help and with no council member around.

If praying is the act of speaking things to be, if praying is an act of talking things to existence, and the Bible was clear that God said, "Let there be..."; it therefore means God prayed or chanted the world to be. And if He said, "Let us make man in our image and likeness", it also means we were made with the ability to speak things forth as His image and likeness. The creation was prayed by God, from God into existence. We as his image must understand that the ability to bring things to being and the ability to make things will come from our original pattern of imagery. God is the maker, the God who prays with Himself, and to Himself. In the New Testament, Jesus restored what we lost in Adam by prayer. That is the reason why the victory at Calvary was not on mount Calvary, the victory at Calvary was won in the garden of Gethsemane. Without a garden of Gethsemane, there could be no victory of the Cross.

CHAPTER
ONE

THE ORIGIN

◆◆◆◆◆◆◆◆◆◆◆◆◆◆◆◆◆◆

Everything that exists has a beginning. There is nothing on this planet that has no beginning. In order to grasp the depth of a thing, the origin has to be explored. As we delve into the matter of prayer, it is incumbent upon us to look at the origin of prayer. However, in order to answer this question, we must ask ourselves some other questions like: "Where did men get the idea of prayer?" We will never understand or know what prayer is all about except man is involved. If men were involved and we resolved that through God we were able to know prayer, the next question then will be, "Where did men come from?" The origin of man can be known through the most authentic and truthful word in the universe, the Holy Bible. The Septuagint (a Greek version of the Hebrew Bible.), documents the origin of humanity. The book of Genesis made it very plain:

Genesis 1:26-28 King James Version (KJV)

> **26** And God said, Let us make man in our image, after our likeness: and let them have dominion over the fish of the sea, and over the fowl of the air, and over the cattle, and over all the earth, and over every creeping thing that creepeth upon the earth.
>
> **27** So God created man in his own image, in the image of God created he him; male and female created he them.
>
> **28** And God blessed them, and God said unto them, Be fruitful, and multiply, and replenish the earth, and subdue it: and have dominion over the fish of the sea, and over the fowl of the air, and over every living thing that moveth upon the earth.

So if man was made in the image and the likeness of God, we must have inherited the DNA of prayer from God. The ability to pray, the way of prayer, making things happen by prayer, and every other issue regarding prayer come from God. I believe that when the Bible said God made this earth, it was actually saying God prayed for this earth to begin. We all agree that prayer means speaking, proclaiming, petitioning, chanting etc. So when the Bible made us understand that God said a lot of 'let there be...' in the book of Genesis, they materialized.

Genesis 1:3-24 King James Version (KJV)

3 And God said, Let there be light: and there was light.

4 And God saw the light, that it was good: and God divided the light from the darkness.

5 And God called the light Day, and the darkness he called Night. And the evening and the morning were the first day.

6 And God said, Let there be a firmament in the midst of the waters, and let it divide the waters from the waters.

7 And God made the firmament, and divided the waters which were under the firmament from the waters which were above the firmament: and it was so.

8 And God called the firmament Heaven. And the evening and the morning were the second day.

9 And God said, Let the waters under the heaven be gathered together unto one place, and let the dry land appear: and it was so.

10 And God called the dry land Earth; and the gathering together of the waters called he Seas: and God saw that it was good.

11 And God said, Let the earth bring forth grass, the herb yielding seed, and the fruit tree yielding fruit after his kind, whose seed is in itself, upon the earth: and it was so.

12 And the earth brought forth grass, and herb yielding seed after his kind, and the tree yielding fruit, whose seed was in itself, after his kind: and God saw that it was good.

13 And the evening and the morning were the third day.

14 And God said, Let there be lights in the firmament of the heaven to divide the day from the night; and let them be for signs, and for seasons, and for days, and years:

15 And let them be for lights in the firmament of the heaven to give light upon the earth: and it was so.

16 And God made two great lights; the greater light to rule the day, and the lesser light to rule the night: he made the stars also.

17 And God set them in the firmament of the heaven to give light upon the earth,

18 And to rule over the day and over the night, and to divide the light from the darkness: and God saw that it was good.

19 And the evening and the morning were the fourth day.

20 And God said, Let the waters bring forth abundantly the moving creature that hath life, and fowl that may fly above the earth in the open firmament of heaven.

21 And God created great whales, and every living creature that moveth, which the waters brought forth abundantly, after their kind, and every winged fowl after his kind: and God saw that it was good.

22 And God blessed them, saying, Be fruitful, and multiply, and fill the waters in the seas, and let fowl multiply in the earth.

23 And the evening and the morning were the fifth day.

24 And God said, Let the earth bring forth the living creature after his kind, cattle, and creeping thing, and beast of the earth after his kind: and it was so.

In all of this story, God created by speaking. God created by the power of His word and proclamation. God created by praying things to be. He decreed things to be, and he prophesied things to be. It will be appropriate to say in the beginning, God prayed for things to be by the power of His word.

Today, if we carry His presence and are positioned like Him, we can decree a thing and it shall come to pass. In the book of Job Twenty-two Verse Twenty-eight, it said, "Thou shalt also decree a thing, and it shall be established unto thee: and the light shall shine upon thy ways." Decreeing a thing is indicative of praying for things to be.

It is also very fascinating that God rested on the seventh day of creation. I have often asked myself what was God really doing.

What is the magnitude of His work that the God of the universe, the God that has all power in His hand, the One who rules the heaven and the earth would need to rest? Well, I would like to submit to you that whatever God was doing that required Him to rest must have been tedious. The reality of prayers must also be viewed in the sense of a hard-working exercise.

If you are an intercessor, you will understand that true prayer drains and saps your strength and energy. So all the 'let there be' of God was a labor of birthing.

God prayed for this world to exist. Even after He made mankind in His image and likeness, He went ahead and breathed Himself into man and man became a living soul. God is a praying God that made man as His image to set an eternal pattern for humanity. It is very clear that it is prayer that made this earth, and it can only be sustained and perpetuated for the glory of God by prayers.

CHAPTER
TWO

THE ADAM
CONNECTION

◆◆◆◆◆◆◆◆◆◆◆◆◆◆◆◆◆◆◆

Adam was designed and placed in Eden, the garden of God to have dominion, multiply, subdue and replenish the earth. We are the imagery of God. As He is in heaven so we are on the earth. God desired a family on the earth like the one He had in heaven. Jesus said, "Thy kingdom come and thy will be done on earth as it is heaven." When God made Adam, He also placed in Adam the DNA that decrees and makes things. Interestingly, to get this thing going, God set up an agreement that became one. He put Adam to sleep to take out the Eve He had kept there. Just as God was pregnant with everything He made on the earth, so was Adam. Just as God pushed them by decree to the earth so were Adam and Eve expected to be pregnant with the vision and birth it. Beloved, God has given us the same imagery so that whatever we want done, if we can conceive it, we can do it. We were made to be objects of prayers. God breathed into man and man became a living soul.

Genesis 2:7-8 King James Version (KJV)

> **7** And the Lord God formed man of the dust of the ground, and breathed into his nostrils the breath of life; and man became a living soul.
>
> **8** And the Lord God planted a garden eastward in Eden; and there he put the man whom he had formed.

It is absolutely fascinating to see God breath into man and man becomes a living soul. Let us not forget that in the New Testament, Jesus also breathed on His disciples. These are processes of prayers. Elijah the prophet breathed on the son of the dead widow in the course of prayers and the boy came alive. I have been instructed many times in the course of praying for people where God wanted me to breathe on the sick and they got healed instantly. Adam had what he needed to make this planet what it is today, and that is the power of prayer. Every invention that has ever been conceived, every progress that has ever been recorded, was made possible because somebody, somewhere prayed. The heavens are not permitted to interfere with the affairs of the earth until the inhabitants of the earth begin to pray. Adam was built and designed to enforce the mandate of God. This mandate is only made possible by the power of prayer.

I have often asked myself this question: "How did Adam name all the animals?" I think that was a great assignment especially if you have to name all the animals below the waters of the earth and the ones in the air. Adam was not just hundred percent human, but he was a living spirit. His living spirit was deposited there by God. I also often ask myself, where Adam got his blood. We must never forget that there is an affinity and synergy in the blood of a man and his breath. God placed all of these things in Adam for a reason.

King David declared in the book of Psalms that we are fearfully and wonderfully made. The history of humanity on this planet is studded with acts of prayers. We must also realize that if we are going to do anything meaningful with our lives on this earth, we must recognize how we got here. The original intent was also revealed because God communicates and fellowships with men. The act of prayer involves communication with God. God had mandated Adam by giving him what it takes to live on his planet.

Adam named everything on this planet by engaging the terrestrial, by engaging the celestial and by engaging the aquatics. Interestingly, all creation is older than man. However, we must not also forget that when God was bringing forth things to occupy this planet we were in God. It will also mean that when God was making the angels we were also in God. No wonder the Bible said we will judge angels. We must come to terms and realize that God has given us everything that calls for life everlasting in Christ Jesus.

Ephesians 1:3-12 King James Version (KJV)

> **3** Blessed be the God and Father of our Lord Jesus Christ, who hath blessed us with all spiritual blessings in heavenly places in Christ:
>
> **4** According as he hath chosen us in him before the foundation of the world, that we should be holy and without blame before him in love:
>
> **5** Having predestinated us unto the adoption of children by Jesus Christ to himself, according to the good pleasure of his will,
>
> **6** To the praise of the glory of his grace, wherein he hath made us accepted in the beloved.
>
> **7** In whom we have redemption through his blood, the forgiveness of sins, according to the riches of his grace;
>
> **8** Wherein he hath abounded toward us in all wisdom and prudence;

9 Having made known unto us the mystery of his will, according to his good pleasure which he hath purposed in himself:

10 That in the dispensation of the fullness of times he might gather together in one all things in Christ, both which are in heaven, and which are on earth; even in him:

11 In whom also we have obtained an inheritance, being predestinated according to the purpose of him who worketh all things after the counsel of his own will:

12 That we should be to the praise of his glory, who first trusted in Christ.

This passage is profound because it opens our eyes to see that God has given us everything we will ever need; all for His glory and honor so that at the fullness of time, He will gather together in one all things in Christ. That is gathering the family in heaven and on the earth so that we can be one. As you read this book, I want you to see how the machinery of the earth was set up by God through the system of prayers. Whatever we are going to become in our life and destiny will be dependent on our attitude towards prayer. It is my prayer that God will open your eyes to see prayer the way God wants you to see it. Don't just pray, but become a prayer yourself.

CHAPTER THREE

MANIFESTATION

◆◆◆◆◆◆◆◆◆◆◆◆◆◆◆◆◆◆

When the Garden of Eden was designed by God, it was designed to be an abode of prayers and worship. The Garden of Eden was designed as an altar of prayer. God will come in the cool of the day to commune with man. One of the questions I often ask myself is, "Where was Adam when the serpent spent a quality time quizzing Eve?" Is it possible that he was somewhere not doing anything? Even when his wife offered him the fruit, couldn't he have prayed and communed with God? If he had communed with God or prayed to God, maybe the disaster would have been avoided. Whenever we surround ourselves and engage in a time of prayer, disaster would often be averted. As we approach the crescendo of human sagacity, we must come to terms that the greatest need of humanity is a heart that can pray until something happens. In the book of Ezekiel, God was keen on finding a man that would stand in the gap so that His people would not be destroyed.

Ezekiel 22:29-31 King James Version (KJV)

> **29** The people of the land have used oppression, and exercised robbery, and have vexed the poor and needy: yea, they have oppressed the stranger wrongfully.
>
> **30** And I sought for a man among them that should make up the hedge, and stand in the gap before me for the land, that I should not destroy it: but I found none.
>
> **31** Therefore have I poured out mine indignation upon them; I have consumed them with the fire of my wrath: their own way have I recompensed upon their heads, saith the Lord God.

There were men and women who throughout the Bible became intercessors. They saved nations, won battles, brought down evil empires, and set the dominion of God on the earth.

Noah single-handedly stood in the gap between the heavens and the earth. He interceded for one hundred and twenty years. Think about how powerful he was as he determined the course of human history.

The generation of Israel would have perished as a Jacob if their ancestor had not taken the bull by the horn. In the book of Genesis, Jacob knew that his past had found him out, he understood how the system of the earth operates by prayer, and he knew he needed to quickly do something so that his posterity would not perish. He therefore went ahead and wrestled in prayer to be changed from Jacob to Israel.

Genesis 32:9-30 King James Version (KJV)

> **9** And Jacob said, O God of my father Abraham, and God of my father Isaac, the Lord which saidst unto me, Return unto thy country, and to thy kindred, and I will deal well with thee:
>
> **10** I am not worthy of the least of all the mercies, and of all the truth, which thou hast shewed unto thy servant; for with my staff I passed over this Jordan; and now I am become two bands.
>
> **11** Deliver me, I pray thee, from the hand of my brother, from the hand of Esau: for I fear him, lest he will come and smite me, and the mother with the children.
>
> **12** And thou saidst, I will surely do thee good, and make thy seed as the sand of the sea, which cannot be numbered for multitude.

13 And he lodged there that same night; and took of that which came to his hand a present for Esau his brother;

14 Two hundred she goats, and twenty he goats, two hundred ewes, and twenty rams,

15 Thirty milch camels with their colts, forty kine, and ten bulls, twenty she asses, and ten foals.

16 And he delivered them into the hand of his servants, every drove by themselves; and said unto his servants, Pass over before me, and put a space betwixt drove and drove.

17 And he commanded the foremost, saying, When Esau my brother meeteth thee, and asketh thee, saying, Whose art thou? and whither goest thou? and whose are these before thee?

18 Then thou shalt say, They be thy servant Jacob's; it is a present sent unto my lord Esau: and, behold, also he is behind us.

19 And so commanded he the second, and the third, and all that followed the droves, saying, On this manner shall ye speak unto Esau, when ye find him.

20 And say ye moreover, Behold, thy servant Jacob is behind us. For he said, I will appease him with the present that goeth before me, and afterward I will see his face; peradventure he will accept of me.

21 So went the present over before him: and himself lodged that night in the company.

22 And he rose up that night, and took his two wives, and his two womenservants, and his eleven sons, and passed over the ford Jabbok.

23 And he took them, and sent them over the brook, and sent over that he had.

24 And Jacob was left alone; and there wrestled a man with him until the breaking of the day.

25 And when he saw that he prevailed not against him, he touched the hollow of his thigh; and the hollow of Jacob's thigh was out of joint, as he wrestled with him.

26 And he said, Let me go, for the day breaketh. And he said, I will not let thee go, except thou bless me.

27 And he said unto him, What is thy name? And he said, Jacob.

28 And he said, Thy name shall be called no more Jacob, but Israel: for as a prince hast thou power with God and with men, and hast prevailed.

29 And Jacob asked him, and said, Tell me, I pray thee, thy name. And he said, Wherefore is it that thou dost ask after my name? And he blessed him there.

30 And Jacob called the name of the place Peniel: for I have seen God face to face, and my life is preserved.

It took an all-night warfare to change Jacob to Israel. There are situations in our lives that can only be resolved by all-night prayers. Remember in this wrestling, Jacob was with God and not with the devil. No wonder Jesus said, "From the days of John the Baptist until now, the kingdom of heaven suffers violence and only the violent can take it by force." In other words, only the forceful can seize it. We must never forget that in the kingdom of God, it has always been so. I believe it is this revelation that will bring revolution to our world.

Moses was a man of prayer that understood the operations of God's government, until God Himself did not want him to pray at some point . In one instance, Moses had gone to Mount Sinai to wait on God. As he waits there for all forty days, the Children of Israel backslide and they ask Aaron to make them a god. Aaron demanded for their earrings and made a golden calf for them to worship. The God that has eyes like fire saw them and told Moses that He had made a decision to wipe them out and raise a new generation through Moses. Interestingly, God told Moses not to pray to Him because His mind was made up.

Exodus 32:1-14 King James Version (KJV)

> **1** And when the people saw that Moses delayed to come down out of the mount, the people gathered themselves

together unto Aaron, and said unto him, Up, make us gods, which shall go before us; for as for this Moses, the man that brought us up out of the land of Egypt, we wot not what is become of him.

2 And Aaron said unto them, Break off the golden earrings, which are in the ears of your wives, of your sons, and of your daughters, and bring them unto me.

3 And all the people brake off the golden earrings which were in their ears, and brought them unto Aaron.

4 And he received them at their hand, and fashioned it with a graving tool, after he had made it a molten calf: and they said, These be thy gods, O Israel, which brought thee up out of the land of Egypt.

5 And when Aaron saw it, he built an altar before it; and Aaron made proclamation, and said, To morrow is a feast to the Lord.

6 And they rose up early on the morrow, and offered burnt offerings, and brought peace offerings; and the people sat down to eat and to drink, and rose up to play.

7 And the Lord said unto Moses, Go, get thee down; for thy people, which thou broughtest out of the land of Egypt, have corrupted themselves:

8 They have turned aside quickly out of the way which I commanded them: they have made them a molten calf, and have worshipped it, and have sacrificed thereunto, and said, These be thy gods, O Israel, which have brought thee up out of the land of Egypt.

9 And the Lord said unto Moses, I have seen this people, and, behold, it is a stiffnecked people:

10 Now therefore let me alone, that my wrath may wax hot against them, and that I may consume them: and I will make of thee a great nation.

11 And Moses besought the Lord his God, and said, Lord, why doth thy wrath wax hot against thy people, which thou hast brought forth out of the land of Egypt with great power, and with a mighty hand?

12 Wherefore should the Egyptians speak, and say, For mischief did he bring them out, to slay them in the mountains, and to consume them from the face of the earth? Turn from thy fierce wrath, and repent of this evil against thy people.

13 Remember Abraham, Isaac, and Israel, thy servants, to whom thou swarest by thine own self, and saidst unto them, I will multiply your seed as the stars of heaven, and all this land that I have spoken of will I give unto your seed, and they shall inherit it forever.

14 And the Lord repented of the evil which he thought to do unto his people.

The question we must ask ourselves about this text is: why did God say to Moses, "Do not pray to me or intercede for them? God knew if Moses were to go into prayer, He would have no choice but to listen to him because of their relationship. Moses held God by His word until he changed the mind of God.

Friends, if you know God in the place of prayer, He will change nations through you. The Word of God declares that those that know their God shall be strong and do exploits. The secret of doing exploits in the kingdom is knowing your God. Moses was a mighty man of prayer that he was able to guide Israel on their journey to resettlement. We all know that when God speaks, it is final, and nobody can alter it. However, Moses changed God's mind through His own word.

Nehemiah was another man of prayer and a consistent intercessor. Israel was in bondage and it seemed like help would never come from anywhere. Nehemiah engaged God in the depths of prayer until he changed the mind of King Artaxerxes, who finally gave them permission to go back to their homeland. The king not only gave them permission, he also financed their trip. There is no limit to what God can do through our prayers.

Nehemiah 1:2-9 King James Version (KJV)

2 That Hanani, one of my brethren, came, he and certain men of Judah; and I asked them concerning the Jews that had escaped, which were left of the captivity, and concerning Jerusalem.

3 And they said unto me, The remnant that are left of the captivity there in the province are in great affliction and reproach: the wall of Jerusalem also is broken down, and the gates thereof are burned with fire.

4 And it came to pass, when I heard these words, that I sat down and wept, and mourned certain days, and fasted, and prayed before the God of heaven,

5 And said, I beseech thee, O Lord God of heaven, the great and terrible God, that keepeth covenant and mercy for them that love him and observe his commandments:

6 Let thine ear now be attentive, and thine eyes open, that thou mayest hear the prayer of thy servant, which I pray before thee now, day and night, for the children of Israel thy servants, and confess the sins of the children of Israel, which we have sinned against thee: both I and my father's house have sinned.

7 We have dealt very corruptly against thee, and have not kept the commandments, nor the statutes, nor the judgments, which thou commandedst thy servant Moses.

8 Remember, I beseech thee, the word that thou commandedst thy servant Moses, saying, If ye transgress, I will scatter you abroad among the nations:

9 But if ye turn unto me, and keep my commandments, and do them; though there were of you cast out unto the uttermost part of the heaven, yet will I gather them from thence, and will bring them unto the place that I have chosen to set my name there.

Even when the walls of Jerusalem were being constructed, Nehemiah was facing great opposition from the persons of Sanballat, Tobias and the Arabians; yet he was not deterred. He was working with his team and praying at the same time. If we continually work in the realm of prayers, we will accomplish great feats for our God.

I know you will readily agree with me that Daniel was a major prophet. He was one of the most powerful intercessors that ever visited the earth in the ancient past. Seventy years after Jeremiah prophesied that Israel was going to go into captivity in Babylon but will return after seventy years. However, seventy years had passed; they were still in captivity. But thank God for an intercessor like Daniel, who stood in the gap. Thank God for Daniel, who warred with the prophetic Word of God through Jeremiah and Israel went back to their land.

Daniel 9:1-21 King James Version (KJV)

9 In the first year of Darius the son of Ahasuerus, of the seed of the Medes, which was made king over the realm of the Chaldesans;

2 In the first year of his reign I Daniel understood by books the number of the years, whereof the word of the Lord came to Jeremiah the prophet, that he would accomplish seventy years in the desolations of Jerusalem.

3 And I set my face unto the Lord God, to seek by prayer and supplications, with fasting, and sackcloth, and ashes:

4 And I prayed unto the Lord my God, and made my confession, and said, O Lord, the great and dreadful God, keeping the covenant and mercy to them that love him, and to them that keep his commandments;

5 We have sinned, and have committed iniquity, and have done wickedly, and have rebelled, even by departing from thy precepts and from thy judgments:

6 Neither have we hearkened unto thy servants the prophets, which spake in thy name to our kings, our princes, and our fathers, and to all the people of the land.

7 O Lord, righteousness belongeth unto thee, but unto us confusion of faces, as at this day; to the men of Judah, and to the inhabitants of Jerusalem, and unto all Israel, that are near, and that are far off, through all the countries whither thou hast driven them, because of their trespass that they have trespassed against thee.

8 O Lord, to us belongeth confusion of face, to our kings, to our princes, and to our fathers, because we have sinned against thee.

9 To the Lord our God belong mercies and forgivenesses, though we have rebelled against him;

10 Neither have we obeyed the voice of the Lord our God, to walk in his laws, which he set before us by his servants the prophets.

11 Yea, all Israel have transgressed thy law, even by departing, that they might not obey thy voice; therefore the curse is poured upon us, and the oath that is written in the law of Moses the servant of God, because we have sinned against him.

12 And he hath confirmed his words, which he spake against us, and against our judges that judged us, by bringing upon us a great evil: for under the whole heaven hath not been done as hath been done upon Jerusalem.

13 As it is written in the law of Moses, all this evil is come upon us: yet made we not our prayer before the Lord our God, that we might turn from our iniquities, and understand thy truth.

14 Therefore hath the Lord watched upon the evil, and brought it upon us: for the Lord our God is righteous in all his works which he doeth: for we obeyed not his voice.

15 And now, O Lord our God, that hast brought thy people forth out of the land of Egypt with a mighty hand, and hast gotten thee renown, as at this day; we have sinned, we have done wickedly.

16 O Lord, according to all thy righteousness, I beseech thee, let thine anger and thy fury be turned away from thy city Jerusalem, thy holy mountain: because for our sins, and for the iniquities of our fathers, Jerusalem and thy people are become a reproach to all that are about us.

17 Now therefore, O our God, hear the prayer of thy servant, and his supplications, and cause thy face to shine upon thy sanctuary that is desolate, for the Lord's sake.

18 O my God, incline thine ear, and hear; open thine eyes, and behold our desolations, and the city which is called by thy name: for we do not present our supplications before thee for our righteousnesses, but for thy great mercies.

19 O Lord, hear; O Lord, forgive; O Lord, hearken and do; defer not, for thine own sake, O my God: for thy city and thy people are called by thy name.

20 And whiles I was speaking, and praying, and confessing my sin and the sin of my people Israel, and presenting my supplication before the Lord my God for the holy mountain of my God;

21 Yea, whiles I was speaking in prayer, even the man Gabriel, whom I had seen in the vision at the beginning, being caused to fly swiftly, touched me about the time of the evening oblation.

My question about this text is, supposing Daniel did not have an understanding to pray, supposing Daniel did not stand in the gap for his nation, they would have been destroyed. Beloved, we are called to war with the prophetic word that God gave to us and we are called to war with those promises that He gave unto us. If God speaks a word to you, you must believe, rest on it and go to war with it. Let us arise and build the city of our God, let us arise and proclaim the gospel of Jesus until He comes again.

CHAPTER FOUR

AS YOU PRAY

◆◆◆◆◆◆◆◆◆◆◆◆◆◆◆◆◆◆

In this chapter, I want you to understand some basic things that are paramount to answered prayers. There are things that are very much fundamental to the 'catchiness' of your prayer before God. If anyone will experience consistent answers to prayers they must understand how it all works. I would like to say to you that God is not obligated to hear your prayer but *His prayer*. That is the reason why an effective prayer is a prayer you pray after you have prayed or praised.

What I mean is that whenever you are getting ready to pray, you must pray to know what to pray for, you must pray to know what God's will is. As you pray, you are able to download from the throne of God, then you will know what is in His heart and what He wants you to pray for; otherwise, you will not be hitting the real target in your prayer.

The prayer that will be answered is also the prayer you pray after you have praised. Starting your prayer with praise will open you up to know the mind of God on what His prayer would be so you might pray for a definite result. Most times prayer can be in the dimension of the outer court, inner court and the Holy of Holies. I believe the pattern of the tabernacle lays credence to our pattern of prayer. There is a spirit, soul, and body of any prayer. You will have to go beyond your selfishness and ego to get to a place of being a true intercessor.

Let us look at the book of First Samuel. Hannah was praying for a child to prove her rival Peninnah wrong, she was praying amiss to prove some point. However, in the midst of desperation mixed with fast and separation, Hannah keys into the 'Holy of Holies' of prayer to know what God's prayer would be. She then prayed for a prophet to redeem Israel from a backslidden condition. That prayer was fired because she returned back to Shiloh with Samuel.

1 Samuel 1:9-20 King James Version (KJV)

> **9** So Hannah rose up after they had eaten in Shiloh, and after they had drunk. Now Eli the priest sat upon a seat by a post of the temple of the Lord.
> **10** And she was in bitterness of soul, and prayed unto the Lord, and wept sore.

11 And she vowed a vow, and said, O Lord of hosts, if thou wilt indeed look on the affliction of thine handmaid, and remember me, and not forget thine handmaid, but wilt give unto thine handmaid a man child, then I will give him unto the Lord all the days of his life, and there shall no razor come upon his head.

12 And it came to pass, as she continued praying before the Lord, that Eli marked her mouth.

13 Now Hannah, she spake in her heart; only her lips moved, but her voice was not heard: therefore Eli thought she had been drunken.

14 And Eli said unto her, How long wilt thou be drunken? put away thy wine from thee.

15 And Hannah answered and said, No, my lord, I am a woman of a sorrowful spirit: I have drunk neither wine nor strong drink, but have poured out my soul before the Lord.

16 Count not thine handmaid for a daughter of Belial: for out of the abundance of my complaint and grief have I spoken hitherto.

17 Then Eli answered and said, Go in peace: and the God of Israel grant thee thy petition that thou hast asked of him.

18 And she said, Let thine handmaid find grace in thy sight. So the woman went her way, and did eat, and her countenance was no more sad.

19 And they rose up in the morning early, and worshipped before the Lord, and returned, and came to their house to Ramah: and Elkanah knew Hannah his wife; and the Lord remembered her.

20 Wherefore it came to pass, when the time was come about after Hannah had conceived, that she bare a son, and called his name Samuel, saying, Because I have asked him of the Lord.

The moment we understand the heart of God in every area of prayers, our testimonies will be guaranteed. As we pray the prayers of God, we should be able to see the answers before we even pray. When we bow our knees, stand or whatever posture we prefer, we must begin to see our answers from the get go. This sight is the eyes of faith. While praying, you should not be distracted by what you see. If you can see your answer after your prayers, you will seize your results. Remember, whatever you can see, you can seize.

We must not only see it, we must also form the thought life and pattern for it. While we are praying we must think it already, then this will be great acts of faith at work. You must not only form the thought life of an answered prayers, we must believe. We must believe that we received. We must be resolute in doubting our doubts, and believe in our beliefs. Jesus made an emphasis of this in the book of Mark Chapter Eleven.

Mark 11:20-26 King James Version (KJV)

> **20** And in the morning, as they passed by, they saw the fig tree dried up from the roots.
>
> **21** And Peter calling to remembrance saith unto him, Master, behold, the fig tree which thou cursedst is withered away.
>
> **22** And Jesus answering saith unto them, Have faith in God.
>
> **23** For verily I say unto you, That whosoever shall say unto this mountain, Be thou removed, and be thou cast into the sea; and shall not doubt in his heart, but shall believe that those things which he saith shall come to pass; he shall have whatsoever he saith.
>
> **24** Therefore I say unto you, What things soever ye desire, when ye pray, believe that ye receive them, and ye shall have them.
>
> **25** And when ye stand praying, forgive, if ye have ought against any: that your Father also which is in heaven may forgive you your trespasses.
>
> **26** But if ye do not forgive, neither will your Father which is in heaven forgive your trespasses.

Jesus said, "If you shall say to this mountain be removed and you don't doubt in your heart, it shall be done." What Jesus was saying is that anything is possible as you pray, believe, and do not doubt in your heart. It is an amazing act of faith.

The night before this incident, Jesus had cursed the fig tree that refused to bring forth fruit. Notice that after He cursed the fig tree, it would seem nothing happened, but in the morning as they passed by, this tree had completely withered. The book of Hebrews says, "Faith Is the substance of things hoped for and the evidence of things not seen." It further said in Verse Six of Hebrews Eleven that: "Without faith, it is impossible to please God. Those that come to him must believe that God is God, and He is a rewarder of them that diligently seek Him."

Another fascinating part of this text (Mark Eleven), was when Jesus spoke about forgiveness. He said, "When you pray, forgive." The question then will be, why did Jesus mention forgiveness at this point? Very simple! Jesus was saying, not forgiving others will hinder our prayers. He even went further by saying, if we come into His presence and we have not forgiven, we must first go and forgive before we can commence our prayers. Beloved, forgiveness is a major conduit for answered prayers.

CHAPTER
FIVE

SETTING THE PATTERN
OF PRAYER

◆◆◆◆◆◆◆◆◆◆◆◆◆◆◆◆◆◆◆

In the historical account of the ministry of Jesus, He gave His disciples a profound pattern of God's kind of prayer. In the synoptic gospel of Matthew, Mark and Luke, Jesus was able to talk to His disciples about definite patterns of prayers. His disciples had watched him come out of prayers to perform wonders, they had seen how prayer was His lifestyle. They had also heard Him teach that men ought to pray and not faint, and also heard him give many parables that lent credence to prayer. They knew John the Baptist taught his disciples how to pray. One day they also appealed to Jesus to teach them how to pray. In the book of Luke Chapter Eleven, Jesus helped His disciples with this request.

Luke 11:1-4 King James Version (KJV)

> **1** And it came to pass, that, as he was praying in a certain place, when he ceased, one of his disciples said unto him, Lord, teach us to pray, as John also taught his disciples.
>
> **2** And he said unto them, When ye pray, say, Our Father which art in heaven, Hallowed be thy name. Thy kingdom come. Thy will be done, as in heaven, so in earth.
>
> **3** Give us day by day our daily bread.
>
> **4** And forgive us our sins; for we also forgive every one that is indebted to us. And lead us not into temptation; but deliver us from evil.

This prayer is popularly referred to as the Lord's Prayer. It is generally accepted in many parts of our world as being the prayer that Jesus wants us to pray, and many books have been printed about it. From childhood, you were made to memorize the Lord's Prayer. Some people even tie it around their neck as if it were a talisman. When Jesus gave us this prayer, it was not meant to be a religious rule. What He did was to give us a pattern of how to pray. Let us look at these patterns in context:

OUR FATHER WHO ART IN HEAVEN

This is the way you start your prayer by acknowledging the Father of creation and of all spirits. Whenever we start our prayer in this fashion, we are simply acknowledging and putting God where He has always been. Not only that, we are also recognizing that we are human and in need of His attention. Jesus wants us to know that we pray to the Father, our father, and we must see it in that context. "Our Father who is in heaven…" It also shows that we serve a God whose abode is in heaven. When we start our prayer recognizing we have a father who is close to us, it builds our confidence, it builds our capacity and also prepares us for everything we are about to say. Remember, we are not just praying to an unknown god or some committee or personality, we are praying to our Heavenly Father.

HALLOWED BE THY NAME

The word *hallow* connotes holy, separate, and reverence. Before we present a request before our Father, it is a perfect thing to revere Him. We need to worship, praise and adore Him knowing there is no other God like him. We cannot just walk into His presence without following His protocol. Like I said in the previous chapter, acknowledging and worshiping Him gives us divine insight into what to pray for, how to pray about it and what strategy is needed for a better result. We must acknowledge and reverence the awesomeness of His majesty.

For those of us who are parents and earthly fathers, we are thrilled when our children come to us in appreciation of who we are in their lives and how much we love them. We normally do not allow them to finish their accolades before we start asking what they will want to eat. My nine year old son knows how to get a pizza from me. He comes to me and gives hugs multiple times to let me know how much he loves me. While he is sweet this way, I will often pick my phone and order him a pizza without him asking me. The pattern that Jesus gave us was to reverence God as we approached His presence.

THY KINGDOM COME.

It is critical and significant for us to understand our priority on planet earth. It is also important to know the role we must play every time we come into the presence of God. It is for the kingdom of God to come. It is for His rule and reign to be established on planet earth. Our job is to pray the kingdom of God down here. When we pray for His kingdom to come, we are setting up a divine platform that we can stand on to place any demand. We often fall short of divine protocol when we do not follow this pattern given to us by our Lord Jesus Christ.

We must therefore pray for His kingdom to come. In our homes, let His kingdom come, in our families, let His kingdom come; in our careers, let His kingdom come in our ministries, let His kingdom come.

THY WILL BE DONE ON EARTH AS IT IS IN HEAVEN

More than anything else, we must pray that God's will be done on earth as it is in heaven. Remember, praying this way will give us the leverage for Him to be involved in what we are petitioning. We need God's involvement because whatever He is involved in cannot be dissolved. We must at all times pray for the will of God to be done on earth as it is in heaven.

All of the documents of the Old and New Testaments are filled with men who did wonders in the name of the Lord because they pursued His will. Take King David as a case study, he sought God's will many times. I carefully used *many times* here because I acknowledge that like many of us, he made some mistakes. But it did not negate the fact that he was so much into God's will that God testified about him being a man after His heart. When we pray, we must pray with the will of God in view. We must, however, ask ourselves what the will of God is.

Beloved, the will of God is the Word of God. Whenever we are praying with His will in our hearts, we are able to pattern all the prayers in the mirror of the Word. The book of Hebrews declares that the Word of God is quick and powerful, sharper than any two-edged sword, piercing to the dividing of asunder, soul, spirit with joints and marrow. It is a discerner of thoughts and intents of the heart. The Word of God is able to separate the soulish prayers from the spirit-led prayers. We must never jump into the presence of God without first praying that His will be done on earth as it is in heaven. As you read this book, pay attention to these truths in your prayer time because they have the propensity to give energy to your prayers.

GIVE US THIS DAY OUR DAILY BREAD

We now come to the crux of this pattern as we begin to make our requests known to God. It is also interesting because this part of the prayer lays emphasis on specifics. It also lays emphasis on one day at a time. I know many people see the word daily bread and they totally misunderstand it. When Jesus put daily bread there, He was pointing to our daily needs. Financial breakthrough could be your daily bread, a happy marriage could be your daily bread, health to your body could be your daily bread, raising your children well could be your daily bread. Whatever that is, your greatest need is your daily bread. God promised us that He will supply all our needs according to His riches in glory by Christ Jesus. In the book of Luke Chapter Eleven, Jesus laid more emphasis on the commitment of God in meeting our daily needs:

Luke 11:5-10 King James Version (KJV)

> **5** And he said unto them, Which of you shall have a friend, and shall go unto him at midnight, and say unto him, Friend, lend me three loaves;

6 For a friend of mine in his journey is come to me, and I have nothing to set before him?

7 And he from within shall answer and say, Trouble me not: the door is now shut, and my children are with me in bed; I cannot rise and give thee.

8 I say unto you, Though he will not rise and give him, because he is his friend, yet because of his importunity he will rise and give him as many as he needeth.

9 And I say unto you, Ask, and it shall be given you; seek, and ye shall find; knock, and it shall be opened unto you.

10 For every one that asketh receiveth; and he that seeketh findeth; and to him that knocketh it shall be opened.

Whenever we raise our voices to God concerning our needs, He does not shut His ears to our requests because He is a good father. He is a prayer answering God. There is absolutely nothing that God will not do for His children. As far as our case is concerned, God is personally involved. He said, "I will be an enemy to your enemy and an adversary to your adversary." He is a God of love, mercy and compassion.

FORGIVE US OUR SINS AS WE FORGIVE OTHERS

This aspect is so pivotal to the result of our prayers. I have often asked people why Jesus would add the clause of forgiveness in this prayer. Simple, He was saying this will be the seed you must sow when you are praying. Forgive those who trespass against you so that your Heavenly Father can forgive you. All of our prayers will be futile if we fail to practice forgiveness. In all of the Gospels, Jesus zeroed in on the essence of forgiveness. We must forgive others just as our Heavenly Father has forgiven us. We must never forget that no matter what others do to us, we have done worse to God and were forgiven. Jesus helps us to understand this better in a parable:

Matthew 18:21-35 King James Version (KJV)

> **21** Then came Peter to him, and said, Lord, how oft shall my brother sin against me, and I forgive him? till seven times?
>
> **22** Jesus saith unto him, I say not unto thee, Until seven times: but, Until seventy times seven.
>
> **23** Therefore is the kingdom of heaven likened unto a certain king, which would take account of his servants.
>
> **24** And when he had begun to reckon, one was brought unto him, which owed him ten thousand talents.
>
> **25** But forasmuch as he had not to pay, his lord commanded him to be sold, and his wife, and children, and all that he had, and payment to be made.

26 The servant therefore fell down, and worshipped him, saying, Lord, have patience with me, and I will pay thee all.

27 Then the lord of that servant was moved with compassion, and loosed him, and forgave him the debt.

28 But the same servant went out, and found one of his fellowservants, which owed him an hundred pence: and he laid hands on him, and took him by the throat, saying, Pay me that thou owest.

29 And his fellowservant fell down at his feet, and besought him, saying, Have patience with me, and I will pay thee all.

30 And he would not: but went and cast him into prison, till he should pay the debt.

31 So when his fellowservants saw what was done, they were very sorry, and came and told unto their lord all that was done.

32 Then his lord, after that he had called him, said unto him, O thou wicked servant, I forgave thee all that debt, because thou desiredst me:

33 Shouldest not thou also have had compassion on thy fellowservant, even as I had pity on thee?

34 And his lord was wroth, and delivered him to the tormentors, till he should pay all that was due unto him.

35 So likewise shall my heavenly Father do also unto you, if ye from your hearts forgive not everyone his brother their trespasses.

Every child of God must pay attention to this parable. If we refuse to forgive those who we think offended us, neither will our Heavenly Father forgive us. Think about how this servant with greater and more grievous offense was let off the hook by his master, yet he refused for somebody else who was less indebted to him to get off the hook. We live in the reality of this parable every day. It is my prayer that we will be filled with the love of Christ to the extent of us being quick and willing to forgive our neighbors.

LEAD US NOT INTO TEMPTATION.

God wants us to pray so that we will not be led into the temptation of sinning against Him. We must first realize that temptation itself is not a sin, falling into temptation is the sin. So what Jesus meant was that we must pray that God will uphold us from sinning against Him. This prayer releases grace into our lives; grace that can teach us to deny ungodliness.

The book of Titus speaks about the grace of God that appeared unto all men that teaches us to deny ungodliness. God has the power to deliver us from sinning against Him.

Something interesting happened in the book of Genesis. Abraham had lied to Abimelech that Sarah, his wife, was his sister. Abimelech did not know and out of ignorance, he took Sarah, the wife of Abraham. However, God appeared to him in a dream and called him a dead man. This king was startled and rattled by this situation and he told God in his dream that he was innocent. God responded by saying, "I understand the integrity of your heart that is why I kept you from sinning against me." So God can keep us from sinning against Him. We must daily pray that God will help us in His awesome grace that we might not sin against Him.

DELIVER US FROM EVIL

What is powerful about this last pattern is the acknowledgment that evil is prevalent in our world, we must therefore pray that God should deliver us from evil. This world that we live in is loaded with evil of every kind. Those who operate with powers from the marine world to suppress others, and those who operate with the powers in the air and the land to perpetrate evil. There is institutionalized evil, there is evil that pervades our world, and evil that seeks to take us from the will of God for our lives.

Apostle Paul acknowledges that even though we walk in the flesh, we do not war after the flesh because our warfare is not carnal but mighty through God to the pulling down of strongholds, casting down imaginations and bringing every thought to the obedience of Christ. Moreover we are ready to avenge all disobedience when our obedience is fulfilled. Jesus said we must pray so that our Heavenly Father can deliver us from evil. Part of the deliverance is God giving us the strategy of staying safe. The scripture in the book of Ephesians Six was very profound:

Ephesians 6:10-18 King James Version (KJV)

> **10** Finally, my brethren, be strong in the Lord, and in the power of his might.
>
> **11** Put on the whole armour of God, that ye may be able to stand against the wiles of the devil.
>
> **12** For we wrestle not against flesh and blood, but against principalities, against powers, against the rulers of the darkness of this world, against spiritual wickedness in high places.
>
> **13** Wherefore take unto you the whole armour of God, that ye may be able to withstand in the evil day, and having done all, to stand.
>
> **14** Stand therefore, having your loins girt about with truth, and having on the breastplate of righteousness;
>
> **15** And your feet shod with the preparation of the gospel of peace;
>
> **16** Above all, taking the shield of faith, wherewith ye shall be able to quench all the fiery darts of the wicked.

17 And take the helmet of salvation, and the sword of the Spirit, which is the word of God:

18 Praying always with all prayer and supplication in the Spirit, and watching thereunto with all perseverance and supplication for all saints;

If we pay attention to the prayer of our deliverance from evil, we will be able to do greater things for our God. Jesus made it very plain in this pattern of prayer that we will be able to come to the fulfillment of everything that God has in store for us if we adhere to it.

CHAPTER
SIX

HINDRANCES TO PRAYERS
◆◆◆◆◆◆◆◆◆◆◆◆◆◆◆◆◆◆◆

W e need to look in the Word of God and see some of the things that might cause hindrances to our prayers. I would like to lay a premise here that it is possible for someone's prayers to be hindered. Notice that I use the word hindrance. There is a difference between being hindered and being totally stopped. Hindrance is indicative of being made slow, experiencing difficulty in advancing, and being delayed. So someone can be delayed but still get their answers with time, if the condition of such delay is changed. There are times in our lives that we put ourselves in positions to be hindered. God had set many laws in motion, a system set by him. This system of God is like the locomotive engine that runs the world. There are certain laws in the spirit, and if you attack these laws, they will fight you. In the book of Isaiah, we see how God was plain about making His people to understand His philosophy concerning this topic.

Isaiah 59:1-10 New King James Version (NKJV)

Separated from God

59

Behold, the Lord's hand is not shortened,

That it cannot save;

Nor His ear heavy,

That it cannot hear.

2

But your iniquities have separated you from your God;

And your sins have hidden *His* face from you,

So that He will not hear.

3

For your hands are defiled with [a]blood,

And your fingers with iniquity;

Your lips have spoken lies,

Your tongue has muttered perversity.

4

No one calls for justice,

Nor does *any* plead for truth.

They trust in empty words and speak lies;

They conceive [b]evil and bring forth iniquity.

5

They hatch vipers' eggs and weave the spider's web;

He who eats of their eggs dies,

And *from* that which is crushed a viper breaks out.

6

Their webs will not become garments,

Nor will they cover themselves with their works;

Their works *are* works of iniquity,

And the act of violence *is* in their hands.

7

Their feet run to evil,

And they make haste to shed innocent blood;

Their thoughts *are* thoughts of iniquity;

Wasting and destruction *are* in their paths.

8

The way of peace they have not known,

And *there is* no justice in their ways;

They have made themselves crooked paths;

Whoever takes that way shall not know peace

God was definite when He spoke to His people about the fact that His ear was not heavy that He could not hear, neither was His hand short that He could not save, but their iniquities had separated them from Him and their sin had also hindered them from Him. If we believe in the validity of this word, it means iniquities and sin can hinder our prayers to God. If we continually live in sin, and stop following Jesus, we can be hindered.

There are many today who question God's goodness because the devil has lied to them. Listen, God has been good to you before you were born and He is still good to you. At times, if you are experiencing delays, you might need to check yourself to find out if you are properly positioned. This does not mean everyone who commits sin will be hindered. If that were so, none of us would be qualified and worthy. What God is pulling out of that text for us is concerning those that reject Jesus. They reject Him in their character, in their speech and actions. We must be properly positioned to receive from God. Being positioned is to be in alignment with Jesus Christ, and being in alignment helps us to know the will of God in our lives.

LIVING IN DOUBT

When we live in doubt, it will be difficult to receive from God. We must doubt our doubts and believe our beliefs. One of the major hindrances to an answered prayer is doubt. Whenever we pray and entertain doubt, it undermines the propensity of a great testimony. We must believe even when we have not seen it. The book of Hebrews Eleven declares that faith is the substance of things hoped for and the evidence of things not seen. It went further to say that by faith, elders before us obtained a good report.

For without faith it is impossible to please God, those that come to Him must believe that God is, and He is a rewarder of them that diligently seek Him. Jesus talks more in the gospel about the danger of doubts, and was a mighty faith preacher even though He was faith himself.

Mark 11:22-24 New King James Version (NKJV)

> **22** So Jesus answered and said to them, have faith in God. **23** For assuredly, I say to you, whoever says to this mountain, 'Be removed and be cast into the sea,' and does not doubt in his heart, but believes that those things he says will be done, he will have whatever he says. **24** Therefore I say to you, whatever things you ask when you pray, believe that you receive *them,* and you will have *them*

If we are going to experience the power of God in answered prayers, we must cast away our doubts and believe in God. It is better to put our confidence in God than to put our confidence in men. Heaven and earth shall pass away but the Word will stand for ever. King David said, "I will lift up my eyes unto the hills, from whence comes my help, our help comes from God, the creator of heaven and the earth. He that keeps Israel will neither sleep nor slumber." Those that put their confidence in God will be like Mount Zion that cannot be moved. If we will pray and do not allow doubts near us, our testimonies will be guaranteed.

WRONG MOTIVE

Apostle James spoke about asking amiss in the book of James. When the Apostle spoke about asking amiss he was referring to having the wrong motive. Sometimes we can experience hindrances because our motives are wrong. There have been times that we spend time praying and it seems like there is no tangible result in sight. We must at that time take a break so we can ask ourselves honest questions. What are we asking from God? Why are we asking and what do we intend to do with what we are asking for? I realize that the answers to all these questions will help us position ourselves properly as we come to God in prayer. Let us look at what James explains to us:

James 4:1-4 King James Version (KJV)

> **4** From whence come wars and fightings among you? Come they not hence, even of your lusts that war in your members?
> **2** Ye lust, and have not: ye kill, and desire to have, and cannot obtain: ye fight and war, yet ye have not, because ye ask not.

3 Ye ask, and receive not, because ye ask amiss, that ye may consume it upon your lusts.

4 Ye adulterers and adulteresses, know ye not that the friendship of the world is enmity with God? whosoever therefore will be a friend of the world is the enemy of God.

If Apostle James, according to the text, speaks about us not receiving because we ask amiss or with the wrong motive, it means he was addressing what was already going on. One of the reasons also for this is because we might have an intention to consume it upon our lusts. Let us not forget that most times, God has to circumcise our hearts so we can know how to ask with the right attitude and motive. It is my prayer that we will pay attention to our motives as we come into the presence of God.

There are many people today that come to God in prayer with a motive of "I just want to get something from God." In essence, they are literally using God, and when they get what they want they tend to stay away from Him until they have another need. God is good and gracious as He still shows mercy to us. However, there are times that He allows delays to reveal our motives. He wants us to focus on Him - the giver, and not the gifts.

MARITAL OBLIGATIONS

How we treat our spouses has the propensity of determining the answers to our prayers. The conditions of a man and his wife help to determine how their prayers are being answered. There are many things we have overlooked sometimes, and those things in most cases have the capacity to derail so many things in our lives. Apostle Peter made it clear in his book:

1 Peter 3:7 King James Version (KJV)

> **7** Likewise, ye husbands, dwell with them according to knowledge, giving honor unto the wife, as unto the weaker vessel, and as being heirs together of the grace of life; that your prayers be not hindered.

The Word of God wants us to deal with our wives wisely so that our prayers will not be hindered. There are many men today who continually dishonor their wives not knowing that God is displeased with it. And if God is displeased, then it might also show in the response to our prayers. It is my ardent prayer that as you read this book, you will pay attention to treating your spouse with honor.

FORGIVENESS

There is nothing more damning to the flow of prayers like lack of forgiveness. Not being able to forgive others is a major hindrance to our prayer life. In most parts of the Bible when Jesus talked about prayer, He never talked about prayer without mentioning forgiveness. The honest question we have to ask ourselves is, why would Jesus end every of His discourse on prayer with forgiveness. Beloved, forgiveness is pivotal and essential to a healthy prayer life. Jesus had this to say:

Mark 11:24-26 King James Version (KJV)

> **24** Therefore I say unto you, What things whatsoever ye desire, when ye pray, believe that ye receive them, and ye shall have them.
>
> **25** And when ye stand praying, forgive, if ye have ought against any: that your Father also which is in heaven may forgive you your trespasses.
>
> **26** But if ye do not forgive, neither will your Father which is in heaven forgive your trespasses.

Forgiveness is the key that unlocks heaven doors during prayers. . Jesus further elaborates that if you bring your gift to the altar and lack forgiveness, you should leave your gift on the altar and go settle the matter before coming to offer your gift. . Being able to forgive others for what they did to us gives us the leverage to present our petition, and God will answer our prayers. Apostle Paul admonishes us that we should be kind to one another, tender-hearted even as God for Christ sake had forgiven us.

CHAPTER
SEVEN

THE DIMENSIONS
OF PRAYERS

◆◆◆◆◆◆◆◆◆◆◆◆◆◆◆◆◆◆◆

We must understand that prayers are not the same. There are dimensions to prayer. If we desire to maximize our time before God and get tangible results, then we need to pay attention to these dimensions. You will agree with me that the word dimension is a mathematical term that connotes measurement and space. In a sense, it is like a parameter. Jesus said in the book of Matthew Chapter Seven:

Matthew 7:7-11 King James Version (KJV)

> 7 Ask, and it shall be given you; seek, and ye shall find; knock, and it shall be opened unto you:
> 8 For every one that asketh receiveth; and he that skeet findeth; and to him that knocketh it shall be opened.

9 Or what man is there of you, whom if his son ask bread, will he give him a stone?

10 Or if he ask a fish, will he give him a serpent?

11 If ye then, being evil, know how to give good gifts unto your children, how much more shall your Father which is in heaven give good things to them that ask him?

There are three main words that stand out in this text. They are: *ask*, *seek* and *knock*. We are going to look at these three words as they relate to what Jesus was talking about. In a previous chapter, I spoke about prayer being viewed in the light of three dimensions: the spirit, the soul and the body. Which can be likened to the outer court, the inner court and the Holy of Holies.

ASKING.

Jesus said, "Ask and it shall be given..." There is a dimension in prayer that resonates from the outside. It is the act of just going ahead to present our petition before God. It is the body aspect of the prayer. Again it also depends on the magnitude of what we are petitioning Him about. Remember Jesus had His reason why He distinctly separated this asking, seeking and knocking.

We need to remember at this point that when Jesus returned from the mount of transfiguration, He met a man whose son was possessed with demons. His disciples had prayed and they could not cast the demons out. Jesus, however, commanded the evil spirits to depart, and they did. But the disciples were concerned why they could not cast out the demons, and Jesus told them that this dimension does not happen except by prayer and fasting. There are times that we go before God in a regular way and under regular circumstances, where we come to the throne of grace to obtain mercy and find grace to help in times of need. And there are other times when we must go the extra mile to obtain what we desire.

Hebrews 4:16 King James Version (KJV)

> **16** Let us therefore come boldly unto the throne of grace, that we may obtain mercy, and find grace to help in time of need.

As we come to the throne of His grace we are able to make our petition before God. Jesus said, whatsoever we ask the Father in His name, we will receive. It is amazing that God laid the protocol of an effective prayer before us. Asking is the basis of prayer and as we believe God, we will receive all that we are asking. The book of John declares that if we ask anything of Him we know He hears us, and if He hears us we shall also receive whatever we ask of Him.

SEEKING

The seeking dimension is different from just the asking. The word to seek means: to resort to, to go in search of, or to try to discover. To seek is to try and discover. Whenever we are at the point of a major situation in our lives. It could be a crisis, some problem, or some real life challenges. We don't just go ahead, pray and say, "By and by, all will be okay." Friends, we must prayerfully seek and find out how we can approach such moments.

Seeking is going before God to first find out what the issue is. After discovering what is wrong, we go ahead and seek how we should pray to have the result that we desire. When we are in the dimension of seeking, we don't just approach God anyhow, we go in to know how it must be done.

The children of Israel at many points in their journey were faced with difficult moments. In all of their battles, God gave them different types of strategies. Until they were able to apply the specific strategy for the specific war, they did not get the victory. When they were confronted with the Egyptian army at the red sea, God told Moses to stretch the rod and the sea was divided. When they got to the water of Meribah, Moses went into prayers and God told him to speak to the rock. However, Moses did not obey which eventually caused him not to enter the promised land. Seeking helps us to know specifics.

Numbers 20:6-12 King James Version (KJV)

6 And Moses and Aaron went from the presence of the assembly unto the door of the tabernacle of the congregation, and they fell upon their faces: and the glory of the Lord appeared unto them.

7 And the Lord spake unto Moses, saying,

8 Take the rod, and gather thou the assembly together, thou, and Aaron thy brother, and speak ye unto the rock before their eyes; and it shall give forth his water, and thou shalt bring forth to them water out of the rock: so thou shalt give the congregation and their beasts drink.

9 And Moses took the rod from before the Lord, as he commanded him.

10 And Moses and Aaron gathered the congregation together before the rock, and he said unto them, Hear now, ye rebels; must we fetch you water out of this rock?

11 And Moses lifted up his hand, and with his rod he smote the rock twice: and the water came out abundantly, and the congregation drank, and their beasts also.

12 And the Lord spake unto Moses and Aaron, Because ye believed me not, to sanctify me in the eyes of the children of Israel, therefore ye shall not bring this congregation into the land which I have given them.

When we get to the area of seeking from God, we are in a dimension that involves deep prayers of inquiry, plans and implementation. Moses and Aaron were in the presence of God where they were able to hear Him and know what the specifics were. However, it became a disaster because Moses did not listen to Him. Instead of speaking to the rock to bring the much needed water, he smote the rock twice and God was displeased.

The seeking dimension of prayer calls for effort, commitment and tenacity. All those that God greatly used in the Bible were not just men who operated from the dimension of asking, they were men who graduated to the realm of seeking in prayers. Daniel sought God with all his heart and was able to have a telescopic prophetic sight about the future of our world. He made an amazing prayer as he sought God:.

Daniel 9:16-23 King James Version (KJV)

> **16** O Lord, according to all thy righteousness, I beseech thee, let thine anger and thy fury be turned away from thy city Jerusalem, thy holy mountain: because for our sins, and for the iniquities of our fathers, Jerusalem and thy people are become a reproach to all that are about us.

17 Now therefore, O our God, hear the prayer of thy servant, and his supplications, and cause thy face to shine upon thy sanctuary that is desolate, for the Lord's sake.

18 O my God, incline thine ear, and hear; open thine eyes, and behold our desolations, and the city which is called by thy name: for we do not present our supplications before thee for our righteousnesses, but for thy great mercies.

19 O Lord, hear; O Lord, forgive; O Lord, hearken and do; defer not, for thine own sake, O my God: for thy city and thy people are called by thy name.

20 And whiles I was speaking, and praying, and confessing my sin and the sin of my people Israel, and presenting my supplication before the Lord my God for the holy mountain of my God;

21 Yea, whiles I was speaking in prayer, even the man Gabriel, whom I had seen in the vision at the beginning, being caused to fly swiftly, touched me about the time of the evening oblation.

22 And he informed me, and talked with me, and said, O Daniel, I am now come forth to give thee skill and understanding.

23 At the beginning of thy supplications the commandment came forth, and I am come to shew thee; for thou art greatly beloved: therefore understand the matter, and consider the vision.

Like Daniel, if we are going to ever make a mark on this earth as it relates to our lives, ministries and our careers, we must be at the dimension of seeking in our prayers.

KNOCKING

The third dimension of prayer is where the prayer is all about God. It is about knowing His purpose and pursuing it in prayer with effort, consistency, and persistency. It is the area of never giving up in prayers. Remember, if you are knocking it takes your cooperation with God. This dimension is where it becomes the last bus stop after discerning what the will of God is. To knock is an act of aggression. To knock is to strike with a sharp blow, to collide with something, to make a pounding noise, or to exert force.

Jesus said, "From the days of John the Baptist until now, the kingdom of heaven suffers violence and only the violent take it by force." The Bible also said, "Elijah was a man of passion like everyone else, but he prayed that it might not rain and it didn't rain for the space of three and a half years; he prayed again, and the rains came." There are men who have walked on this planet, and through the power of prayer and intercession had brought the glory of God down. Elijah refused to get up from his knees until it rained. These were men who continually prayed until something happened.

1 Kings 18:41-45 King James Version (KJV)

41 And Elijah said unto Ahab, Get thee up, eat and drink; for there is a sound of abundance of rain.

42 So Ahab went up to eat and to drink. And Elijah went up to the top of Carmel; and he cast himself down upon the earth, and put his face between his knees,

43 And said to his servant, Go up now, look toward the sea. And he went up, and looked, and said, There is nothing. And he said, Go again seven times.

44 And it came to pass at the seventh time, that he said, Behold, there ariseth a little cloud out of the sea, like a man's hand. And he said, Go up, say unto Ahab, Prepare thy chariot, and get thee down that the rain stop thee not.

45 And it came to pass in the mean while, that the heaven was black with clouds and wind, and there was a great rain. And Ahab rode, and went to Jezreel.

What differentiates Elijah from other prophets was his tenacity and persistence in prayers. In the book of Daniel, when Daniel began to pray, the Prince of Persia withstood him. However, he refused to leave his place of prayer until the answer came. We in our day must go the extra mile to accomplish things for our God.

In the early hours of January 11, 1992, I walked through Gurley Street in the city of Monrovia, Liberia, and had an experience that I will never forget for the rest of my life. As an evangelist, I had spent time praying for more souls to be saved in the nation of Liberia, when God woke me up one morning and led me to the worst ghetto in the nation. My experience on this day became like a burning bush experience.

When I arrived at this ghetto, I saw hundreds of young people, especially teenagers, hooked on drugs. There was noise everywhere, people buying and selling cocaine, marijuana and heroin. Some of them were lying down sick after being wounded by those who caught them stealing. I stood in the midst of this pandemonium and cried for almost an hour. They were surprised and wondered what was wrong with me. I could not say anything. I walked out of the place knowing that I had to do something about it. But as I left, I could also hear the voice of the devil saying, "You can't come here, this is my territory." When I got home that afternoon. God began to open my eyes to a scripture in the book of Luke:

Luke 11:21-22 King James Version (KJV)

> **21** When a strong man armed keepeth his palace, his goods are in peace:

22 But when a stronger than he shall come upon him, and overcome him, he taketh from him all his armor wherein he trusted, and divided his spoils.

When I read this passage, I told God if you will anoint me, I will go to that territory and get them saved. I did not come out of my room that day. I took a fast and went into prayers because Jesus said, "Knock, and the door shall be opened." I was determined to knock on the door for the anointing needed to minister to this type of people. I was determined not to drink or eat until I heard from God. On the eighth day of my fasting and praying before God, He told me, "Go, for I have given you the territory and the souls in it." The rest is history today because the worst ghetto in the nation of Liberia became home to one of the fastest growing Churches in the nation. Many of those who were bound by drugs and involved in heinous crimes became senators, congressmen and women, business tycoons, bishops and pastors, and great women who are building the economy of Liberia. Friends, this could only happen by cooperating with God in His redemptive plan for Liberia and our world. As you read this book, it is my prayer and challenge to you to knock on heaven's door; God will hear you and make a name out of you.

CHAPTER EIGHT

SPIRITUAL WARFARE

❖❖❖❖❖❖❖❖❖❖❖❖❖❖❖❖❖

The biggest battle on this planet today is not the one in Iraq, it is not the one in the Darfur region of Sudan, nor the one between Isis and the Western world. The battle we are faced with today is the battle for the souls of men. It is the tussle between the malevolent power of evil and the benevolent power of good. No matter how we try to talk it away and rationalize things through the technological advancement of our time, spiritual warfare is real. We must first realize that it is not the physical that establishes the spiritual.

Genesis 1 King James Version (KJV)

> **1** In the beginning God created heaven and the earth.
> **2** And the earth was without form, and void; and darkness was upon the face of the deep. And the Spirit of God moved upon the face of the waters.

3 And God said, Let there be light: and there was light

We know from this text that the Spirit moved first. It was the Spirit that went into operation before anything was made.

It is the spiritual that establishes the physical. Without the spiritual, the physical cannot hold, and if the spiritual is not established, the physical cannot exist.

We have two forces that are operational on this earth. We have the benevolence power of good that comes from God, the malevolent power of evil that comes from Satan. As humans on this planet, we are caught between these two worlds. The place where we stay and lean on will determine how much victory we enjoy. Dominion and authority was given to us in the Garden of Eden.

Genesis 1:26-28 King James Version (KJV)

> **26** And God said, Let us make man in our image, after our likeness: and let them have dominion over the fish of the sea, and over the fowl of the air, and over the cattle, and over all the earth, and over every creeping thing that creepeth upon the earth.
> **27** So God created man in his own image, in the image of God created he him; male and female created he them.

28 And God blessed them, and God said unto them, Be fruitful, and multiply, and replenish the earth, and subdue it: and have dominion over the fish of the sea, and over the fowl of the air, and over every living thing that moveth upon the earth.

After God gave us all we needed and became the custodians for this earth, there was an interruption. We mortgaged and relinquished our authority to Satan. The rest of the story in the Bible after Genesis Chapter Three, is the story of our redemption. Two thousand and some hundred years ago, a man by the name of Jesus was born in the city of Bethlehem. Wrapped in the flesh of a virgin named Mary, He was the perfect Lamb of God to redeem us from the sins of the world.

John 3:16 King James Version (KJV)

16 For God so loved the world, that he gave his only begotten Son, that whosoever believeth in him should not perish, but have everlasting life.

The Bible declares that while we were still sinners Christ died for us. From the beginning, God gave us the capability to pray things through. The capability to dominate, subdue and replenish the earth. It is embedded in the DNA of God for us. We lost it in Adam, but Jesus gave it back to us. Whatever we lost in the first

Adam, the second and the last Adam gave it back to us. When man fell in the Garden of Eden, he went into a spiritual coma until Jesus restored us to the original Edenic plan. Jesus is the best thing that ever happened on this planet. Apostle John laid it out clearly in his opening chapter:

John 1:1-15 King James Version (KJV)

> **1** In the beginning was the Word, and the Word was with God, and the Word was God.
>
> **2** The same was in the beginning with God.
>
> **3** All things were made by him; and without him was not any thing made that was made.
>
> **4** In him was life; and the life was the light of men.
>
> **5** And the light shineth in darkness; and the darkness comprehended it not.
>
> **6** There was a man sent from God, whose name was John.
>
> **7** The same came for a witness, to bear witness of the Light, that all men through him might believe.
>
> **8** He was not that Light, but was sent to bear witness of that Light.
>
> **9** That was the true Light, which lighteth every man that cometh into the world.
>
> **10** He was in the world, and the world was made by him, and the world knew him not.

11 He came unto his own, and his own received him not.

12 But as many as received him, to them gave he power to become the sons of God, even to them that believe on his name:

13 Which were born, not of blood, nor of the will of the flesh, nor of the will of man, but of God.

14 And the Word was made flesh, and dwelt among us, (and we beheld his glory, the glory as of the only begotten of the Father,) full of grace and truth.

Jesus, who is God, showed us throughout the gospel the power of prayer. From all indications, He showed us how He got things done. He was a definite praying machine. We must never forget that everything written in the Bible is written for our good. Whatever Jesus did when He was physically here for those thirty-three years was done for our good. He taught us spiritual warfare and how to live a victorious life. The Bible gives many instances how Jesus started His day through spiritual warfare and prayers.

Mark 1:35 King James Version (KJV)

35 And in the morning, rising up a great while before day, he went out, and departed into a solitary place, and there prayed.

COMMANDING THE DAY

The act of rising early to raise an altar of prayer to God started from the day of creation. All our ancestors that God raised to change our world from Prophet Adam through Enoch, from Enoch through Noah, from Noah through Abraham we saw how they exercised the dominion that God gave them. In the New Testament, we also see how Jesus was an early morning riser. If we are going to fulfill the mandate of God, we must be ready to wake up early in the morning, commanding the day. Let us see what God expects of us through the eyes of the oldest book of the Bible. In Job Thirty-eight, God asked Job some interesting questions:

Job 38:12-13 King James Version (KJV)

> **12** Hast thou commanded the morning since thy days; and caused the dayspring to know his place;
> **13** That it might take hold of the ends of the earth, that the wicked might be shaken out of it?

God was asking Job if he had commanded the morning. Why, because that is one of the reasons God planted us on this earth, and to have dominion over the fish of the sea, the fowls of the air and over everything that creeps upon the earth. The dominion mandate is made possible as we wake up to set God's dominion around us.

We are clothed with the authority to determine how our day must look, if we quit ignorance and embrace the knowledge of God. Remember, the word of God declares that those that know their God will be strong and they will do exploits. We can therefore command our world in prayer; for Jesus said, "Whatever we bind on earth shall be bound in heaven and whatever we lose on earth shall be loosed in heaven."

The other part of that passage speaks about us commanding the morning and causing the dayspring to know its place. Why must the dayspring know its place?, So that it might take hold of the ends of the earth, that the wicked might be shaken out of it. We must wake up daily to do a consistent spiritual warfare and engage in prayers through binding the wicked spirits to keep them away and render them powerless. We must attack and subdue wicked spirits daily so that God's will may be done on this planet. Apostle Paul talks about our spiritual warfare in Ephesians Chapter Six:

Ephesians 6:10-18 King James Version (KJV)

> **10** Finally, my brethren, be strong in the Lord, and in the power of his might.
> **11** Put on the whole armour of God, that ye may be able to stand against the wiles of the devil.

12 For we wrestle not against flesh and blood, but against principalities, against powers, against the rulers of the darkness of this world, against spiritual wickedness in high places.

13 Wherefore take unto you the whole armour of God, that ye may be able to withstand in the evil day, and having done all, to stand.

14 Stand therefore, having your loins girt about with truth, and having on the breastplate of righteousness;

15 And your feet shod with the preparation of the gospel of peace;

16 Above all, taking the shield of faith, wherewith ye shall be able to quench all the fiery darts of the wicked.

17 And take the helmet of salvation, and the sword of the Spirit, which is the word of God:

18 Praying always with all prayer and supplication in the Spirit, and watching thereunto with all perseverance and supplication for all saints.

Beloved we are at war, we are in the midst of powers that do not want us to succeed in the purpose that God has set apart concerning our destiny. We must, as a matter of urgency, arise and command the day. We decide how we want our day to be through consistent prayers and spiritual warfare. Let us not forget the night controls the day and above controls beneath. If you cannot wake up to control the night, you will waste the day. If you cannot control the power of the heavenly bodies in the early hours, you will not be able to control it in the day.

Most spirits are activated to operate in the night, and once it is getting to day, they resort to their abode where they are not able to function properly because of their jurisdiction. We must not forget that the time the enemy declares fierce battle is not in the day, but at night. We must not also forget that all our activities on the earth are dictated by the heavens. When it gets dark the sons of men resort to rest, when it is cold from up there we change our apparels. Why are we doing this? Because our dictates come from above. If we are going to control the earth, we must control it from above.

KEEP BACK THE WEIGHT

If we want to become warriors for our God, we must be ready to resist every evil weight throughout the day. In the course of the day, the evil spirits will try to manipulate us by getting us so engrossed in our activities that we barely lift our heads to acknowledge our maker. There are different kinds of weights that the enemy might use on us so we need to be prayerful.

Sometimes it could come by stifling our zeal for the things of God. If we are not consciously resisting him, it could linger on until it becomes a disaster. At other times, the weight could come in the form of oppression or depression. We just suddenly become depressed for no reason and might start feeling sorry for ourselves. These are the works of evil spirits. That is the reason why if we have any bad dreams, we must pray them away from us. Prayer and consistent spiritual warfare are part of the ways to keep you free.

Evil spirits will do what they can to steal from you and keep you restricted throughout the day. You therefore have to understand that, "The weapons of our warfare are not carnal, but they are mighty through God to the pulling down of strongholds and casting down imaginations, and bringing into captivity every thought to the obedience of Christ; and having in a readiness to revenge all disobedience when your obedience is fulfilled." (2 Corinthians 10:4-6)

Sometimes evil spirits might roll the weight of guilt upon us. They sometimes make us guilty for no reason. If you have done wrong and you go to God in repentance, God will forgive you because there is power in the blood of Jesus. After you are forgiven, evil spirits will do all they can to make you feel guilty and doubt God's forgiveness; do not listen to their lies.. Stand on God's Word and rebuke those voices to maintain your freedom. Apostle John declares that, "This is the message we bring unto you that God is light, and in Him there is no darkness at all." (1 John 1:5).

If we walk in the light as He is in the light, we have fellowship with one another and the blood of Jesus Christ cleanses us from every sin. In Galatians Five, Paul admonishes us to stand in the liberty wherewith Christ has made us free. Jesus said, "He who the Son sets free, is free indeed."

CREATING ORDER

One of the major reasons why we must be prayerful and engaged in spiritual warfare is to create order around us. Part of the mandate that God left for us on this planet is to create order. An order for the free flow of God's manifestation and power. We are made for the glory of God, and without order, we cannot do or accomplish much.

Think about it, God could do nothing until He created order from the chaos around. The earth was without form and void, and darkness was upon the face of the deep, and the spirit of God moved upon the face of the waters and God said, "Let there be light, and there was light." The presence of light was an order to the chaos and darkness. Whether in the night or in the day time, we must engage the spiritual realm so that we can keep the order of God. We must create order to set the dominion of God on the earth. We must daily pierce the cloud with prayers and shatter evil plans of the enemy. There are many lives, many families, homes, and communities today that are in chaos. Our job is to create the order of Jesus in all these areas. We are the light of the world and the salt of this earth; we are a city set on a hill that cannot be hidden. Wherever God has placed you, He wants you to rule and reign there.

Many years ago, before my mission to the United States, I lived in a very beautiful community. There was a major street that led to the road to my community. At this junction, ghastly - and sometimes, fatal accidents were a monthly occurrence. One day I woke up with a deep burden to do something about these occurrences. I walked to the junction and spent some time praying over it. After that prayer, the accidents stopped. We are called by God to create order in a chaotic world. Until a child of God rises and does something about the prevailing evil in our world, nothing will happen. We must stop the evil around us by creating order. It is time to set the dominion of God on the earth. Only a prevailing prayer can stop a prevailing evil.

CHAPTER NINE

THE DISCIPLINE OF PRAYER

◆◆◆◆◆◆◆◆◆◆◆◆◆◆◆◆◆◆◆◆

If we will be effective in our prayer lives, we must be disciplined. Only people who are disciplined can effectively pray. Prayer has nothing to do with your feelings, it is a way of life. If we are disciplined to make prayer a way of life, we will bring changes to our world. Normally, our body will not like to pray. Our body cannot stand the supernatural for too long. Having said this, we must also remember that intercession is hard work. However, if it becomes a way of life, it becomes pleasurable. If we are going to engage in a result-oriented prayer, we cannot afford to be distracted. There are times that we are not focused, and at such times, we seldom get the required results. Praying involves discipline and persistence. . The Bible is filled with men who were audacious enough to pray, and through their prayers God shook the foundations of the earth.

The first thing we must do is to make a decision. Prayers must be borne out of the decision we make whether to pray or not. Everything starts from the point of making a decision. Our decisions define our attitude towards life. There are many times that our bodies are tired and we do not feel like praying, but as we force ourselves by our decision to pray, we suddenly realize that we are strengthened. Too often, the flesh loves to cooperate with the devil to distract us from praying.

The next thing is, we must be determined to pray. Our determination is a great conduit to our growth in prayer and spiritual warfare. Jesus said in the book of Matthew: "From the days of John the Baptist until now the kingdom of heaven suffers violence, and only the violent take it by force." In the book of Luke Chapter Eighteen, Jesus gave a profound parable.

Luke 18:1-8 King James Version (KJV)

> **18** And he spake a parable unto them to this end, that men ought always to pray, and not to faint;
> **2** Saying, There was in a city a judge, which feared not God, neither regarded man:
> **3** And there was a widow in that city; and she came unto him, saying, Avenge me of mine adversary.

4 And he would not for a while: but afterward he said within himself, Though I fear not God, nor regard man;

5 Yet because this widow troubleth me, I will avenge her, lest by her continual coming she weary me.

6 And the Lord said, Hear what the unjust judge saith.

7 And shall not God avenge his own elect, which cry day and night unto him, though he bear long with them?

8 I tell you that he will avenge them speedily. Nevertheless when the Son of man cometh, shall he find faith on the earth?

The woman in this text was so determined that she refused to give up, she persistently went to the Judge for revenge. Initially the judge had turned her down, but as she persisted, he had no choice but to answer her request. To all of these, Jesus admonished us to pray and not faint. What is fascinating in this text is Jesus telling us not to faint. If He is telling us not to faint, it means we have the tendency of fainting.

Discipline entails us raising an altar wherever we are so that we can continually communicate with God. Discipline means sometimes having specific hours we meet God daily. That hour cannot be replaced by anything. The hour of prayer is the hour of life, the hour of prayer is the hour of deliverance. Not getting up to pray is tantamount to a death sentence. If we refuse to stand in the hour prayer, we might be captured by the wicked. We do not have a choice, as this is a case of no retreat or surrender. We are called to discipline ourselves to prayers. Apostle James drew the analysis of prayer in virtually everything we do.

James 5:13-18 King James Version (KJV)

> **13** Is any among you afflicted? let him pray. Is any merry? let him sing psalms.
>
> **14** Is any sick among you? Let him call for the elders of the church; and let them pray over him, anointing him with oil in the name of the Lord:
>
> **15** And the prayer of faith shall save the sick, and the Lord shall raise him up; and if he have committed sins, they shall be forgiven him.
>
> **16** Confess your faults one to another, and pray one for another, that ye may be healed. The effectual fervent prayer of a righteous man availeth much.
>
> **17** Elias was a man subject to like passions as we are, and he prayed earnestly that it might not rain: and it rained not on the earth by the space of three years and six months.
>
> **18** And he prayed again, and the heaven gave rain, and the earth brought forth her fruit.

Like Elijah, we are men and women of like passion, but we can also discipline ourselves to pray until something happens. Many years ago Evangelist Billy Graham was asked to list his three most needed tools for his evangelistic tour. His list had prayer as number one, two and three. Beloved, Prayer is a major currency of heaven and prayer is the key that unlocks heaven doors. Apostle Paul admonishes us to pray without ceasing. One of the habits we must cultivate is to be prayer-minded. Once we are prayer-minded, we will pray all the time. It means if our mind is full of prayer, we will pray. Beloved, as you read this book, remember we cannot pray enough. You will often hear people say, "I have been praying and I think I have prayed enough." No, the day you eventually come out with the thought that you have been praying enough, is the day you know you have not been praying. Wherever you are in the world, you can set up an altar of prayer. Whether you are cooking, driving, or flying thousands of feet in the air, there is always somewhere available for a quick prayer. Interestingly many restrooms are warfare rooms.

A Few years back when I was an evangelist and following up on new converts, I had an experience that has been imprinted in my heart. I had gone to visit a family where the wife was already saved but the husband had not yet given his life to Christ. What was unfortunate about that day was when I got to this house, the man and his wife happened to be in a fight. It was not just verbal, but an altercation. . As I walked into the house, the Lord opened my eyes, and I noticed that there was a creature in the house that was not allowing the gospel of Jesus to have pre-eminence. In the midst of their quarrel, I tried talking to them but they paid me no attention. At this point, I asked to use their restroom. When I entered their restroom I prayed for three minutes. As soon as I came out, they both apologized for the embarrassment. The big testimony was the man telling me that he wanted to give his life to Christ and he got saved that day. Twenty-two years have gone by and they are still serving God together. Glory to God! Beloved, supposing I did not address this enemy of God, they probably would have been in that situation with no help. In the book of Acts, Paul had to deal with Elymas so the power of the gospel could flow freely.

Acts 13:5-12 King James Version (KJV)

> **5** And when they were at Salamis, they preached the word of God in the synagogues of the Jews: and they had also John to their minister.
> **6** And when they had gone through the isle unto Paphos, they found a certain sorcerer, a false prophet, a Jew, whose name was Barjesus:

7 Which was with the deputy of the country, Sergius Paulus, a prudent man; who called for Barnabas and Saul, and desired to hear the word of God.

8 But Elymas the sorcerer (for so is his name by interpretation) withstood them, seeking to turn away the deputy from the faith.

9 Then Saul, (who also is called Paul,) filled with the Holy Ghost, set his eyes on him.

10 And said, O full of all subtlety and all mischief, thou child of the devil, thou enemy of all righteousness, wilt thou not cease to pervert the right ways of the Lord?

11 And now, behold, the hand of the Lord is upon thee, and thou shalt be blind, not seeing the sun for a season. And immediately there fell on him a mist and a darkness; and he went about seeking some to lead him by the hand.

12 Then the deputy, when he saw what was done, believed, being astonished at the doctrine of the Lord.

Beloved, there are many Elymas today in our lives, ministries, and careers. Our assignment from God is to shut them down by the power of prayer. This type of prayer is only possible if we are willing to discipline ourselves and stay in His presence. Let us therefore arise, and go forth in the power of His might through prayers, to take territories for our God.

CHAPTER
TEN

EFFECTIVE PRAYER
◆◆◆◆◆◆◆◆◆◆◆◆◆◆◆◆◆◆

God is not obligated to answer our prayers. What makes our prayer effective is understanding the heart of God on what to pray for when we decide to pray. That is the reason why we pray and praise to know what to pray for. Jesus said, "When you pray, say: Our Father who art in heaven, hallowed be thy name..." Hallowing God grants us access to know what to pray for. There are many ways laid out in the Word of God to pray effective prayers. All those who left legacies in the Bible were men and women who through effective prayers subdued kingdoms, conquered enemies, raised the dead, and survived persecutions from tyrannical rulers.

WORD-BASED PRAYERS.

Whenever the foundation of our prayers is rooted in the Word of God, the results are astounding. If you go into the Word of God to pull out your prayers, you are no longer praying your prayer but praying God's prayer. There is something about the Word of God that will make anything possible. The writer of the book of Hebrews said, "The Word of God is powerful, and sharper than any two-edged sword, piercing even to the dividing asunder of soul and spirit, joints and marrow. It is a discerner of thoughts and intents of the heart.

Whenever we speak God's word back to Him, we are setting ourselves up for a testimony. He said, "My word that goes forth, it will not return to me void, it will accomplish its purpose and prosper wherever it is sent."

God needed Joshua to understand that if he were to ever succeed in the new position that was transferred to him by Moses, he would need to stay with the Word. He said to him, "This book of the law shall not depart out of your mouth, but you shall meditate on it day and night so you can observe to do all that is written therein and you shall make your way prosperous and have a good success."

The devil can fight your ideas, he can even fight your philosophy, but he cannot fight the Word of God. Jeremiah declares that the Word of God is a fire, it is a hammer that breaks rocks to pieces. Isaiah the prophet said, "The grass will wither and the flower will fade away, but the Word will stand forever." David the king, also affirmed that the Word of God is a lamp unto our feet and a light to our paths, and forever God's word is settled in heaven. Beloved, praying word-based prayer is praying God's prayer.

PRAYERS MIXED WITH FASTING

Prayers that are mixed with fasting are very effective. Fasting does not change God, but it changes us by making us have a laser focus and increase our level of sensitivity. The prayer we make while fasting has high energy and a propensity for speed. There are some things that will only change through fasting. In the Old Testament, greater feats of God were performed by men and women who understood the benefits of fasting. We would never have had the Torah or the Ten Commandments today if Moses did not go to Mount Sinai with fasting and prayer to God. In the book of Esther, the future of Israel was hanging in the balance, the posterity of the Jewish race was under the threat of annihilation. Mordecai was alerted, and he communicated the message to his niece, Esther - who had become a queen by heaven orchestration. Under the difficult circumstances of meeting the king at an odd hour, she requested a fast from her people so she could approach the king for the salvation of her people.

Esther 4:1-16 King James Version (KJV)

4 When Mordecai perceived all that was done, Mordecai rent his clothes, and put on sackcloth with ashes, and went out into the midst of the city, and cried with a loud and a bitter cry;

2 And came even before the king's gate: for none might enter into the king's gate clothed with sackcloth.

3 And in every province, wherever the king's commandment and his decree came, there was great mourning among the Jews, and fasting, and weeping, and wailing; and many lay in sackcloth and ashes.

4 So Esther's maids and her chamberlains came and told . Then was the queen exceedingly grieved; and she sent raiment to clothe Mordecai, and to take away his sackcloth from him: but he received it not.

5 Then called Esther for Hatach, one of the king's chamberlains, whom he had appointed to attend upon her, and gave him a commandment to Mordecai, to know what it was, and why it was.

6 So Hatch went forth to Mordecai unto the street of the city, which was before the king's gate.

7 And Mordecai told him of all that had happened unto him, and of the sum of the money that Haman had promised to pay to the king's treasuries for the Jews, to destroy them.

8 Also he gave him the copy of the writing of the decree that was given at Shushan to destroy them, to shew it unto Esther, and to declare it unto her, and to charge her that she should go in unto the king, to make supplication unto him, and to make request before him for her people.

9 And Hatach came and told Esther the words of Mordecai.

10 Again Esther spake unto Hatch, and gave him commandment unto Mordecai;

11 All the king's servants, and the people of the king's provinces, do know, that whosoever, whether man or women, shall come unto the king into the inner court, who is not called, there is one law of his to put him to death, except such to whom the king shall hold out the golden sceptre, that he may live: but I have not been called to come in unto the king these thirty days.

12 And they told Mordecai Esther's words.

13 Then Mordecai commanded to answer Esther, Think not with thyself that thou shalt escape in the king's house, more than all the Jews.

14 For if thou altogether holdest thy peace at this time, then shall there enlargement and deliverance arise to the Jews from another place; but thou and thy father's house shall be destroyed: and who knoweth whether thou art come to the kingdom for such a time as this?

15 Then Esther bade them return Mordecai this answer,

16 Go, gather together all the Jews that are present in Shushan, and fast ye for me, and neither eat nor drink three days, night or day: I also and my maidens will fast likewise; and so will I go in unto the king, which is not according to the law: and if I perish, I perish.

Remember in this text that Esther requested for a fast as a backup, as she fasted also. At the end of this fast, she approached the king and the king granted her request. There is power generated whenever we take time out in fasting and prayer.

Fasting and prayer are so significant that Jesus greatly emphasized the need for it. Jesus did not just allude to it, He became the example of it. Think about it, Jesus did not start his full ministry until he had fasted and prayed for forty days and forty nights. My question has always been, why did Jesus need to fast for forty days before embarking on the journey of His ministry. Simple, there are some major events in our lives that will require fasting and prayers. When they needed to separate Paul and Barnabas for the full work of their ministry, the disciples took time out to fast and pray.

Let us look at the occurrence in the book of Mark Chapter Nine where Jesus laid emphasis on the premise of fasting and prayer:

Mark 9:17-29 King James Version (KJV)

17 And one of the multitude answered and said, Master, I have brought unto thee my son, which hath a dumb spirit;

18 And wheresoever he taketh him, he teareth him: and he foameth, and gnasheth with his teeth, and pineth away: and I spake to thy disciples that they should cast him out; and they could not.

19 He answereth him, and saith, O faithless generation, how long shall I be with you? how long shall I suffer you? bring him unto me.

20 And they brought him unto him: and when he saw him, straightway the spirit tare him; and he fell on the ground, and wallowed foaming.

21 And he asked his father, How long is it ago since this came unto him? And he said, Of a child.

22 And ofttimes it hath cast him into the fire, and into the waters, to destroy him: but if thou canst do any thing, have compassion on us, and help us.

23 Jesus said unto him, If thou canst believe, all things are possible to him that believeth.

24 And straightway the father of the child cried out, and said with tears, Lord, I believe; help thou mine unbelief.

25 When Jesus saw that the people came running together, he rebuked the foul spirit, saying unto him, Thou dumb and deaf spirit, I charge thee, come out of him, and enter no more into him.

26 And the spirit cried, and rent him sore, and came out of him: and he was as one dead; insomuch that many said, He is dead.

27 But Jesus took him by the hand, and lifted him up; and he arose.

28 And when he was come into the house, his disciples asked him privately, Why could not we cast him out?

29 And he said unto them, This kind can come forth by nothing, but by prayer and fasting.

The disciples of Jesus could not cast out the devil from the child that was brought to them. They tried hard and it did not work. However, Jesus showed and made it easier by commanding the devils to depart from the child. The disciples were so flabbergasted that they were bent on knowing why they could not cast the demons out of the child. Jesus told them this type of power manifestation cannot happen except by fasting and prayer. Jesus used the word "but", this kind does not happen except by fasting and prayer. Beloved, there are many kinds of things in our lives, families, careers, and in our future, that can only be handled by fasting and prayers.

PRAYING IN TONGUES

One of the ways of praying effective prayers is by praying in tongues. Whenever we pray in tongues we are unleashing the power of God to answer our requests. This is one area of prayer that many believers have not tapped into. Four hundred and fifty years before Jesus was born, Isaiah prophesied that, "With stammering lips and another tongue will he speak to his people." On the day of Pentecost, the power of tongues was released as a sign to what will become a love letter between men and God.

Acts 2:1-4 King James Version (KJV)

> **2** And when the day of Pentecost was fully come, they were all with one accord in one place.
>
> **2** And suddenly there came a sound from heaven as of a rushing mighty wind, and it filled all the house where they were sitting.
>
> **3** And there appeared unto them cloven tongues like as of fire, and it sat upon each of them.

4 And they were all filled with the Holy Ghost, and began to speak with other tongues, as the Spirit gave them utterance.

After the initial baptism of the Holy Spirit, the disciples continued in the power of this tongue. Paul the Apostle admonishes us to pray in tongues. There are times that when we pray, the enemy hears what we are saying and goes ahead to counter and hinder us from receiving our answers. But when we pray in tongues, the devil cannot understand what we are saying, but the God that gave the tongues understands what the spirit is saying. If you pray in tongues, God will decide what your spirit is saying and the answers are quick.

Romans 8:26-27 King James Version (KJV)

26 Likewise the Spirit also helpeth our infirmities: for we know not what we should pray for as we ought: but the Spirit itself makes intercession for us with groanings which cannot be uttered.

·**27** And he that searcheth the hearts knoweth what is the mind of the Spirit, because he maketh intercession for the saints according to the will of God.

Jude 1: 20 King James Version (KJV)

> **20** But ye, beloved, building up yourselves on your most holy faith, praying in the Holy Ghost,

We must seek and desire to pray more in tongues so we can place ourselves in a better position of result-oriented prayers.

TIMES AND SEASON

God is a God of times and seasons. God made times and seasons yet He is not controlled by them. Understanding times and seasons with God is very significant. Whenever we understand the positioning of times and seasons we are able to buy into the mind of God on what to pray for and expect great results. There is something about timing and season that lends credence to the activities of God in the galaxy of the universe. Solomon was the wisest king that ever lived on the earth. He said there are time and season for everything,

To everything there is a season and a time to every purpose under the heaven:

> A time to be born, and a time to die; a time to plant, and a time to pluck up that which is planted;

A time to kill, and a time to heal; a time to break down, and a time to build up;

A time to weep, and a time to laugh; a time to mourn, and a time to dance;

A time to cast away stones, and a time to gather stones together; a time to embrace, and a time to refrain from embracing; time to get, and a time to lose; a time to keep, and a time to cast away;

A time to rend, and a time to sew; a time to keep silence, and a time to speak;

A time to love, and a time to hate; a time of war, and a time of peace. (Ecclesiastes 3:1-8)

Solomon went further to say that, "The race is not to the swift nor the battle to the strong, nor bread to the wise, nor favor to the men of skill, nor riches to men of understanding but time and chance happen to them all." The power of prayer is determined by our understanding of times and seasons.

Jacob had twelve boys and one girl. One among his boys was Issachar. The generation of Issachar were men who understood the signs of time. Because they understood the signs of time and what to do, they were in command of their brothers. Only those who understand times and seasons will have a command in the place of prayers.

Our forefathers in ancient times understood the power of signs, times, and seasons. Because of their understanding, they were able to pray effective prayers that rearranged the destiny of men and nations.

The attitude of Haman in the book of Esther was very interesting. Haman who was the right-hand man of King Ahasuerus. He was going to take permission to exterminate the Jews. Before he walked to the king to seek this permission, he navigated in the realm of the spirit to find how the heavenly bodies will be shifted and what season must be in place. He definitely figured out that if he could just consult his oracles by casting lot or voting everyday, then his request would be granted. Interestingly, when he did enough consulting for a year, the king agreed to the killing of all the Jews. He consulted demonic powers and paid money towards it.

Esther 3:7-9 King James Version (KJV)

> 7 In the first month, that is, the month Nisan, in the twelfth year of king Ahasuerus, they cast Pur, that is, the lot, before Haman from day to day, and from month to month, to the twelfth month, that is, the month Adar.

8 And Haman said unto king Ahasuerus, There is a certain people scattered abroad and dispersed among the people in all the provinces of thy kingdom; and their laws are diverse from all people; neither keep they the king's laws: therefore it is not for the king's profit to suffer them.

9 If it pleases the king, let it be written that they may be destroyed: and I will pay ten thousand talents of silver to the hands of those that have the charge of the business, to bring it into the king's treasuries.

Haman knew when the time and season was ripe for a request to be made to the king for the killing of the Jews. As true watchmen and intercessors, we must seek to understand what the heavens are saying. We must remember that heaven is always speaking. Our job is to find out what it is saying. As we find out what heaven is saying, we can key in to pray to enforce the mind of God.

Psalm 19:1-4 King James Version (KJV)

19 The heavens declare the glory of God; and the firmament sheweth his handywork.

2 Day unto day uttereth speech, and night unto night sheweth knowledge.

3 There is no speech nor language, where their voice is not heard.

4 Their line is gone out through all the earth, and their words to the end of the world. In them hath he set a tabernacle for the sun.

It is our job as the present- day sons of Issachar to buy into the mind of God so we can set the dominion of God on the earth. As we download what God's mind is per season, then we can perform His counsel. In the book of Matthew Chapter Two, we see the wise men as they decoded the counsel of eternity by noticing the differences in the appearance of the stars. The stars and the season announced Jesus, the stars and the season led them to Jesus, and the stars and the season instructed them on what to do. Only wise men of God pay attention to times and seasons in their prayer lives.

One of the saddest things about this age is that the church has allowed the demonic world to manipulate the constellation and nature against them. We must arise as God's people and seize the moment to set God's dominion on the earth.

MATHEMATICAL SYNERGY

We must understand that one of the languages of the spirit is calculus. God communicates with numbers. We must know how to launch forth our prayers strategically. I once met an army personnel who told me everything that made him a name in the army were strategies. Making strategic planning during wars will determine your victory. As we pray, we must take numbers into consideration. There are numbers that play a role in the realm of the spirit.

There is a reason why God rested on the seventh day signifying His number of rest. There is a reason why God kept eight souls in the ark signifying a new beginning. There is also a reason why men were made on the sixth day, signifying the number of men, a number that the devil is always interested in; is it a wonder, therefore, why the mark of the beast for men will be 666? There is a reason why most releases of God's gifts are always nine, no wonder women carry their gift for nine months in the belly. There is a reason why one is beginning. There is a reason why two has always been the agreement number of God. There is also a reason why God is strategic about three, three is a number of resurrection and number four is perfect balance. Covenant is always revealed in twelve. Jacob had twelve boys and Jesus chose twelve disciples for a reason.

Elijah also understood the power of these numbers when he was getting ready to pray on Mount Carmel to call the fire down, he chose twelve stones according to the number of the tribes of Israel. We must study to log into strategic numbers as it applies to our prayers.

Many years ago, I was confronted with a situation where a dead child was brought to my house. I prayed and prayed, nothing happened until God said to me command him to arise three times according to my number of resurrection. I did and the dead child came alive. To God be the glory!

Some of the alignment numbers that come in calendars are not coincidental. Watchmen need to learn and make use of them. There are alignments and synergy that could benefit nations if we seek to understand how they work. Heaven is always speaking. Every year has a gate, every month has a gate, and every week has a gate. We must learn to pray for these gates to be opened. If we consider all of these patterns, we can have guaranteed testimonies. Let us not just pray, let us pray strategically.

APPROPRIATING NATURE AND THE CONSTELLATION

The body of Christ around the world needs a wake-up call to align with God in making use of the authority He has given to us. From the beginning of the book of Genesis, God gave us a mandate that we must enforce. Genesis 1:26-28 King James Version (KJV)

> **26** And God said, Let us make man in our image, after our likeness: and let them have dominion over the fish of the sea, and over the fowl of the air, and over the cattle, and

over all the earth, and over every creeping thing that creepeth upon the earth.

27 So God created man in his own image, in the image of God created he him; male and female created he them.

28 And God blessed them, and God said unto them, be fruitful, and multiply, and replenish the earth, and subdue it: and have dominion over the fish of the sea, and over the fowl of the air, and over every living thing that moveth upon the earth.

The mandate that God gave here was definitely astounding. God gave men dominion over the aquatic, over the celestial and over all the terrestrial. In the book of Job, we also see how God in His conversation with Job, revealed His mind about us making use of the authority that He has given to us. We will be able to know in the book of Job Chapter Thirty-eight, how God thinks towards us and how His counsel concerning our partnership with Him should look like.

Job 38 King James Version (KJV)

38 Then the Lord answered Job out of the whirlwind, and said,

2 Who is this that darkeneth counsel by words without knowledge?

3 Gird up now thy loins like a man; for I will demand of thee, and answer thou me.

4 Where wast thou when I laid the foundations of the earth? declare, if thou hast understanding.

5 Who hath laid the measures thereof, if thou knowest? or who hath stretched the line upon it?

6 Whereupon are the foundations thereof fastened? or who laid the corner stone thereof;

7 When the morning stars sang together, and all the sons of God shouted for joy?

8 Or who shut up the sea with doors, when it brake forth, as if it had issued out of the womb?

9 When I made the cloud the garment thereof, and thick darkness a swaddlingband for it,

10 And brake up for it my decreed place, and set bars and doors,

11 And said, Hitherto shalt thou come, but no further: and here shall thy proud waves be stayed?

12 Hast thou commanded the morning since thy days; and caused the dayspring to know his place;

13 That it might take hold of the ends of the earth, that the wicked might be shaken out of it?

14 It is turned as clay to the seal; and they stand as a garment.

15 And from the wicked their light is withholden, and the high arm shall be broken.

16 Hast thou entered into the springs of the sea? or hast thou walked in the search of the depth?

17 Have the gates of death been opened unto thee? or hast thou seen the doors of the shadow of death?

18 Hast thou perceived the breadth of the earth? declare if thou knowest it all.

19 Where is the way where light dwelleth? and as for darkness, where is the place thereof,

20 That thou shouldest take it to the bound thereof, and that thou shouldest know the paths to the house thereof?

21 Knowest thou it, because thou wast then born? or because the number of thy days is great?

22 Hast thou entered into the treasures of the snow? or hast thou seen the treasures of the hail,

23 Which I have reserved against the time of trouble, against the day of battle and war?

24 By what way is the light parted, which scattereth the east wind upon the earth?

25 Who hath divided a watercourse for the overflowing of waters, or a way for the lightning of thunder;

26 To cause it to rain on the earth, where no man is; on the wilderness, wherein there is no man;

27 To satisfy the desolate and waste ground; and to cause the bud of the tender herb to spring forth?

28 Hath the rain a father? or who hath begotten the drops of dew?

29 Out of whose womb came the ice? and the hoary frost of heaven, who hath gendered it?

30 The waters are hid as with a stone, and the face of the deep is frozen.

31 Canst thou bind the sweet influences of Pleiades, or loose the bands of Orion?

32 Canst thou bring forth Mazzaroth in his season? or canst thou guide Arcturus with his sons?

33 Knowest thou the ordinances of heaven? canst thou set the dominion thereof in the earth?

34 Canst thou lift up thy voice to the clouds, that abundance of waters may cover thee?

35 Canst thou send lightnings, that they may go and say unto thee, Here we are.

In the rhetorical questions God threw at Job, we are able to deduce the mind and counsel of God. We are also able to pull out some prayer points that God is directing us to. While we are looking at this passage, we must never forget that there were many questions in the mind of Job and his friends. When God responded to these questions, He also responded with questions that brought clarity. God asked Job out of the whirlwind if he knew him who darkened counsel by his word, or he that keeps and reveals secrets?

What God is saying is, I am the one that keeps things hidden in matters of prayer and reveals them for my pleasure. God asked Job where he was when He laid the foundation of the earth. Indicating that God laid the foundations in the earth by laying the measures and stretching the lines.

The greatness of God was shown through the reactions of His family in heaven when the sons of God shouted for joy and the morning stars sang together. God further asked Job who shut up the sea with doors when it broke forth as if it issued out of the womb.

From this verse, we were able to know that God has invisible doors that shut the seas in. There is a good prayer point here against those who go into the sea to obtain evil powers to afflict others. So whenever demonic agents go into the sea, we must always pray so that the door should shut against them. We can pray against marine spirits by shutting them in the sea. God has given us weapons of war in the days of battle. He also asked Job if he had commanded the morning and caused the dayspring to speak. I spoke extensively about us commanding the morning in the previous chapter of this book. If God asked Job if he had commanded the morning, it therefore means he could command the morning and if Job could, so can we.

We can wake up daily commanding the dayspring to know its place, that it might take hold of the ends of the earth, and that the wicked might be shaken out of it. God further asked Job if the gates of death had been opened unto him and if he had seen the shadow. It is interesting here because we have a confirmation of Psalm Twenty-three that death has a shadow. It is significant here for us to know that we have the power to command death.

As a student with Dr. Cunningham's Youth With A Mission School, I would go out of campus sometimes to preach in so many other meetings where I was invited. In one of those meetings, something happened that has helped to shape the minister that I am today.

It was an outdoor crusade. As I was getting ready to preach, a woman interrupted the meeting by bringing a dead child to the service. She was crying at the top of her voice, causing more crowds to gather in the meeting. As a young preacher, I was so confused and frightened that I did not know what to do. Somehow I walked to her and took the child and started praying. No matter how I prayed, nothing happened. But as I persisted in my prayer, the Holy Spirit spoke to me and reminded me of this text. He told me to command the spirit of death to let go of his grip over the child. I laid the child on the wide pulpit that I was using and commanded the spirit of death to leave. As I stood over the body, I commanded the spirit of death to leave and the child came back alive. Glory to God!

When we buy into the revelatory secrets of God, our prayers become effective and powerful.

It is also fascinating that God made mention of the constellation of Pleiades, Orion,s belt, Mazzarroth, and Arturus with his sons. We must realize at this point that these constellations have a lot to do with the destiny of humanity. First of all, all of the constellations of the universe are under the command of God. They cooperate with God to accomplish His purpose on the planet earth. There are the sweet influences that could be manipulated, Orion is a cluster of stars held by the chains of God. We can let go of the bounds of Orion to carry out the mandate of God in our lives and nations. Mazzaroth is a constellation that has its season, and we can pull him out to declare the glory or shut down the enemies of God through prayers. We could also guide the constellation of Arturus with his sons by prayers to set the dominion of God on the earth. Everything that God made is subject to His word and as we speak His counsel in prayer, we can be in command of the many constellations in the universe. Many occults and wicked agents of darkness have always manipulated nature and constellations to perpetrate wickedness on the earth. We must rise in the power of Jesus Christ and fight for the glory of our God.

Everything that God made reflects His glory. Everything that God made is also subjected to His voice. We can create forms, decorum and platforms to put nature to work. The sun, the moon, the wind and the stars are all subjected to the word of the living God. We have been given authority on this planet to do the works of God. The Bible declares, "The whole creation awaits the manifestation of the sons of God." Psalms One Hundred and Twenty-one is profound.

Psalm 121:6-7

King James Version

> **6** The sun shall not smite thee by day, nor the moon by night.
> **7** The Lord shall preserve thee from all evil: he shall preserve thy soul.

From this text, we were able to know that the sun and the moon have power to smite. There are people today whose stability is often activated by the appearances of the moon. Demonic agents had worked with their master Satan, for centuries to afflict people through the manipulation of these objects. We must rise to the occasion by punishing every disobedience once our obedience is fulfilled. As we travel through the Bible, we can see how men and women who understood the supernatural shook kingdoms for the glory of God. Joshua understood how this worked and commanded the sun to stand still.

King James Version

Joshua 10:12-13

> **12** Then spake Joshua to the Lord in the day when the Lord delivered up the Amorites before the children of Israel, and he said in the sight of Israel, Sun, stand thou still upon Gibeon; and thou, Moon, in the valley of Ajalon.
>
> **13** And the sun stood still, and the moon stayed, until the people had avenged themselves upon their enemies. Is not this written in the book of Jasher? So the sun stood still in the midst of heaven, and hasted not to go down about a whole day.

When Israel was faced with an intense battle in the book of Judges, the stars in their courses fought against Sisera.

Judges 5:19-20

> **19** The kings came and fought, then fought the kings of Canaan in Taanach by the waters of Megiddo; they took no gain of money.
>
> **20** They fought from heaven; the stars in their courses fought against Sisera.

Understanding the activities of the constellation helps us to pray effectively. In order to get a perfect understanding of the constellation, we must labor in the study of God's Word. If we labor in the Word, God will grant us divine access to the secrets of His truths. If we understand seasons we will be able to open the gates of the seasons. If we understand heaven's pattern, we are able to create patterns. As we draw closer to the end of this age, we are faced with a world that is still not fully prepared for the coming of the Messiah -Jesus Christ. We must be prepared to make major sacrifices from the womb of prayer to usher in the arrival and the second coming of our Lord Jesus Christ. There has never been a time like now where we must rise in the place of Prayer to set the dominion of God on Earth. As you read this book, it is my prayer that you will avail yourself as an intercessor for the redemption of our world. Let us drive out the darkness of the nations and switch on the light of Jesus in the womb of prayers.

EPILOGUE

◆◆◆◆◆◆◆◆◆◆◆◆◆◆◆◆◆◆◆

When we began the journey of prayers from this book, we delved into the origin of prayer. The question was how humanity got the idea of prayer. Where did the tendency for prayer come from? We were able to conclude that God is the God of prayer, therefore our DNA for prayer comes from God because we were made in His image. We realize that God spoke the world to being, so He prayed for the world to be, Adam therefore, perpetuated the legacy of God by becoming the custodian of creation. The means by which he did this was through prayer. He enforced divine mandate by determining and naming things from the sea, the air and the land.

We were also able to look at the manifestations of God's chosen servants through the means of prayer. Jacob became Israel by prayers, Moses saved Israelites from the wrath of God by intercession, and Nehemiah rebuilt the wall of Jerusalem by prayers. Even while Nehemiah and his men were working, they were praying at the same time. Daniel the prophet refused to leave the place of prayer until deliverance came for them.

In Chapter four we saw clearly that God is not obligated to hear our prayers except His own prayer. Therefore it is our duty to pray before praying. There are also patterns in prayer. Jesus taught us how we can pray. In the Lord's Prayer, we were able to see God's pattern. Jesus did not just want us to make the Lord's Prayer a religious magical wand, but an opportunity to know how to pray.

As we explored the details of prayers from this book, we also highlighted that there are possible hindrances to prayer. Doubt, wrong motives and not being willing to forgive could hinder our prayers. Interestingly, Jesus often spoke about forgiveness whenever He talked about prayers. The same thing with his disciples, they made an emphasis on forgiveness. James spoke also about wrong motives too.

In this book, we were also able to see that there are dimensions in prayers. There is the asking dimension, there is the seeking dimension and there is the knocking dimension. All of these prepare us for spiritual warfare in prayers. The greatest battle in our world today is not physical but spiritual. This book teaches us spiritual warfare on how to create order on this earth and how to command the things that are not, as though they existed.

As we close the curtains on this book, we realize that it takes discipline to be a man and woman of prayer. Especially in managing our time and becoming sensitive. To pray an effective prayer, we must pray Word-based prayers. The Word of God must be our foundational stone of prayer. Our prayer is energized also as we mix it with fasting. Somewhere in the book of Mark, Jesus said certain things do not go except by fasting and prayers. Praying in tongues also has a great benefit in yielding greater results. Lastly, praying with an understanding of times, season and the movement of the constellation is a major part of a result-oriented prayer. It is my prayer that you will become a frontline soldier of Christ. I pray that you will become an intercessor with advanced knowledge of the technicalities and the modus operandi of prayers.

Made in the USA
Middletown, DE
03 November 2021

51631733R00078